Making of the Popular

Production of Culture and Discourses in Bangladesh

Manosh Chowdhury
Jahangirnagar University

Series in Anthropology

Copyright © 2025 Vernon Press, an imprint of Vernon Art and Science Inc, on behalf of the author.

All rights reserved. No part of this publication may be reproduced, stored in a retrieval system, or transmitted in any form or by any means, electronic, mechanical, photocopying, recording, or otherwise, without the prior permission of Vernon Art and Science Inc.

www.vernonpress.com

In the Americas:
Vernon Press
1000 N West Street, Suite 1200
Wilmington, Delaware, 19801
United States

In the rest of the world:
Vernon Press
C/Sancti Espiritu 17,
Malaga, 29006
Spain

Series in Anthropology

Library of Congress Control Number: 2025930963

DOI: 10.54094/b-c718eb8ea5

ISBN: 979-8-8819-0228-5

Also available: 979-8-8819-0226-1 [Hardback]; 979-8-8819-0227-8 [PDF, E-Book]

Cover by Anisuzzaman Sohel

Product and company names mentioned in this work are the trademarks of their respective owners. While every care has been taken in preparing this work, neither the authors nor Vernon Art and Science Inc. may be held responsible for any loss or damage caused or alleged to be caused directly or indirectly by the information contained in it.

Every effort has been made to trace all copyright holders, but if any have been inadvertently overlooked the publisher will be pleased to include any necessary credits in any subsequent reprint or edition.

*The outstanding mentor
with unparallel insight and pervasive vision*
Professor Burhanuddin Khan Jahangir

Table of contents

	Preface and Acknowledgement	vii
	List of Acronyms	ix
Chapter 1	Introduction: Location of the 'Popular'	1
Chapter 2	The Zia Manifestation	17
Chapter 3	Nation as a Mode of Consumption	25
Chapter 4	The Politics of Secularism	39
Chapter 5	'Lawful' Heroes and 'Terrorist' Villains	53
Chapter 6	Environmentalism as a Global Consciousness	71
Chapter 7	The Power of Translation	87
Chapter 8	Conclusion: Will Popular Be 'Popular' Again?	101
	References	109

Preface and Acknowledgement

Right after the Covid-19 reconfiguration of leisure, livelihood, and lives, and right after I digitally 'met' Carmen Blyth, an independent author and researcher, I wished (fantasized more precisely) to have several English products under my belt. Finding Carmen was not a coincidence; at least, this is exactly what cyberspace is propagated for. In this case, it is truthful to say that she found me, a very unlikely event in human history, especially when I hardly wrote anything significant in English by that date. Her search (for a random me) coincided with perhaps a few less important issues, and I started nurturing my wish. So, I kept on sending 'mini' proposals to many publishers. Nobody should be surprised to know that most of them were turned down, a good thing about 'corporate' (forget about the University Press tags where applicable, well they maintain a similar bureaucracy, too) publishers is that they 'respond', something their 'left-leaning' counterparts do not even bother to. I happily kept on resending and re-resending them to other publishers once I received an email (with a no, of course). A complete list could irritate even the calmest of readers.

Now, my readers deserve to know that I have a serious 'bias' toward the 'left-leaning' publishers, even knowing the fact of their apparent snobbery or inefficiency. So, my hunt for many publishers for many products naturally involved a few left-leaning publishers, too. And it took an unnecessarily longer time because of the simple fact that I could not even receive a 'no' after waiting for months. In the whole process, the only 'mini proposal' that was accepted in the first attempt was a book roughly about or around films, scheduled to be published by the same publisher. I kept on missing deadlines and rescheduling them again. I never started writing that 'imagined book'. As I started feeling the heat, I was about to tell the publisher to abandon the contract instead. In the process, I started realizing that I needed to publish this manuscript first, or at least to sign a contract for this one to sensibly move forward for anything I wish (or fantasize). I wrote two lines about this manuscript and let the contact person know. I was advised to send a formal proposal. It worked, and this is how this years-old manuscript is getting published.

Why do many publishers turn down a book proposal, or, in many other cases, do not even respond to a query, and, in an ever-growing tendency, ask the authors to find what they define as 'acquisitions editors', or regional editors by some other agencies, and make things far more complicated for an author, especially from the Global South, let alone an author like me who never approached writing in English, is altogether an academic query to me, and needs serious investigation. The first and foremost reason is a simple one – the big agencies have numerous requests to respond to, and they need to discourage many 'unsolicited submissions'. The second reason, however, is not that simple and involves the disparity and hierarchy in the publishing industry in defining the probable authors. It goes further when we consider the ever-growing principles of the academic global order in a tightly scrutinized and almost monolingual fashion. Things are much more complicated when it comes to journal publication tendencies and differ significantly in hard and natural sciences or applied and business (and commerce-related) disciplines. But until and unless the global superstar academics start talking over these issues (especially the prejudices and disparity), these may be groaning by a newcomer in the field.

That I had started writing solely in the local language, Bangla more precisely, in a very early stage of my career, in 1995, has nothing to do directly with the global scenario I am now much concerned about. It was not felt this way back then to be honest. I rather wanted a strong base of social studies in the local language. I came from a small-town Bangla medium secondary school and could have played a bit, but only a bit. It was a pedagogical outlet that I then thought of upholding. And I wrote a lot in the local language. Still, this manuscript, or a version of it, should and could have been published long back, but never it was, due to a series of mundane and interesting stories. For a few years, I thought of publishing it from a local study circle publisher led by an unbelievably capable professor. Then, the study group was struggling with personnel and finance. I then decided to publish its Bangla translation and never found the impetus to translate it by myself into Bangla. Then I shelved it for years only to have a wake-up call during the Covid-19 period, as I told you earlier. So, Carmen Blyth deserves my first gratitude.

The first version of this manuscript was my doctoral dissertation. My doctoral journey has some other stories, too, but I will not burden this preface with my biographic notes. The study was possible under the MEXT scholarship scheme of the government of Japan. I thank the authority for offering me a graduate scholarship during 2004-2007. Professor Masahiko Togawa, my supervisor, found a friendly and non-confronting way to deal with his first-ever doctoral student. I thank him for his relaxed approach to me. Arpana Awwal, a creative teacher of English literature, took care of my English at a time when I could not do any justice to her service. Also, I am grateful to my (Bangla) readers and publishers. They are not many in numbers, but they are crucial for me in keeping my focus for these long years. After all, I am not believed as an easygoing author for the readers.

Manosh Chowdhury
Adabor, Dhaka, Bangladesh
27 December 2023

List of Acronyms

AIDS	Acquired Immunodeficiency Syndrome
BANBEIS	Bangladesh Bureau of Educational Information and Statistics
BAPA	Bangladesh Poribesh Andolon (Bangladesh Environment Movement)
BAT	British American Tobacco
BBC	British Broadcasting Corporation
BELA	Bangladesh Environmental Lawyers Association
BJP	Bharatiya Janata Party
BTC	Bangladesh Tobacco Company
BTV	Bangladesh Television
BNP	Bangladesh Nationalist Party
CHT	Chittagong Hill Tracts
CNN	Cable News Network
CPB	Communist Party of Bangladesh
FCTC	Framework Convention on Tobacco Control
FDC	Film Development Corporation
HBO	Home Box Office
HIV	Human Immunodeficiency Virus
ICS	Islami Chhatra Shibir
ISA	Ideological State Apparatus
JI	Jamaat-e-Islami
NAM	Non-Alliance Movement
NGO	Non-government Organization
OIC	Organization of Islamic Countries
RSA	Repressive State Apparatus
SQC	Salahuddin Quader Chowdhury
UGC	University Grants Commission
UNICEF	United Nations Children's Fund
WHO	World Health Organization

Chapter 1

Introduction: Location of the 'Popular'

This book is about the popularizing project[1] in Bangladesh. That is, how some specific forms of cultural products[2] and some discourses[3] are being constructed and propagated as popular. Contested meanings of popular culture seem to be one of the leading queries during the investigation of this research. At the same time, I also looked at different polarities from which different perspectives – i.e.,

---

[1] The term 'project' is used in reference to the nuances it involves in the social scientific genre of the contemporary age. Besides the conventional usage for a planned program – in business or scientific enterprises, this also entails the deliberate set of acts and ideas that tend towards a particular objective. Often, this specific use conveys the objectives along with the programs. In this body of work, the use of the concept could be compared in parallel to the following uses:
    a)   In title: "Tibi, B. 1995: Culture and Knowledge: The Politics of Islamization of Knowledge as a Postmodern Project? The Fundamentalist Claim to De-Westernization. Theory, Culture & Society, 12, 1."
    b)   In discussion: "....It was the westernization project and the westernizers that led to the breakup of the late Ottoman Empire; it was a westernization project and westernizers that were responsible for the exploitation of the country, its backwardness and poverty of the people as well as cultural alienation of the people from their own civilization" (Dagi 2002).

[2] By cultural products, I mean the relatively familiar broadcast and performed forms of artistic practices like movies, books, or advertising materials along with ideas and intellectual exercises like education curriculum or iconographic political propaganda.

[3] Unlike the common reference to the conversation or utterances, discourse here is used in particular reference to its use in the contemporary social sciences and humanities. "If the analytical value of some terms derives from their descriptive precision and specificity of meaning, other words – such as discourse – owe their utility to multiple layers of meaning and their ability to stimulate ambiguity" (Barnard and Spencer 1996, 162). Within anthropology, along with some other disciplines, discourse has become a crucial concept whereas discursive analysis appeared as one of the influential methodological venture. The kind of "discourse analysis, associated with cultural studies, takes discourse more globally to refer particular areas of language use. This approach blurs together three levels of meaning: discourse is the act of talking or writing itself; it is a body of knowledge content; and it is a set of conditions and procedures that regulate how people appropriately may communicate and use that knowledge. Rather than the elemental structures of conventional interaction, this... approach to discourse pursues the connections between orders of communication, knowledge and power." (Barnard and Spencer 1996, 162-63).

pro-people or elite – regarding forms of popular cultures could be revealed apparently. In the present multifaceted representational context of cultural products, discourses are barely dissociable from culture. Against these backdrops, my 'research' was grounded in various complex and contested domains of popular culture and discourses, and examined the processes of production of those. The central queries were: how the 'popular' is being constructed; how the organs are active in the process of construction, with a mission of 'popularizing'; and how in turn these manifest an overriding sense of 'national-popular' culture. My investigation, intermingled with primary goals, sought to explore relationships among the agents – i.e., film companies, audio-visual companies, corporate financial groups, governmental agencies, educational establishments, middle-class audiences and so on – of the project and between the different social classes in regards to popular culture and discourses.

The Agents and the Issues

As a newly independent nation-state, Bangladesh has a colonial history like most of the Southern nations. The first government after the independence from Pakistan through a deadly fight in 1971, the Awami League government, opted for a gross nationalization of the industries. It included most of the industrial productions like jute, sugar, railways, electricity, and a lot more. Apart from the sectors that are defined as 'economic', as such, sectors of intellectual productions such as textbooks, television programs, radio programs, and extra-curriculum books were also subjected to the incorporation to a modest degree. So, the cultural production, though not solely, was a part of the governmental activities.

Since 1971, radio and television were solely state-owned until the mid-90s. Television was meant to be a single-channel broadcast only for some hours daily. In the last few years, satellite television has provided a lot more visual productions and distributions, both from the local end and from the transnational manufacturers, especially from India. Since the early 90s, satellite television has meant to be the most influential medium of entertainment, across the social classes, including the poor people in the metropolises. Along with the shift in economic policy, from what was then perceived as nationalization to what is currently being promoted as privatization, satellite television provided a huge space for the advertising industry.

Print publications in Bangladesh were always meant to be the shared area for governmental and private ventures. For the first few years after independence in 1971, only a few daily newspapers were in publication and with tight scrutiny from the government end. Secondary and higher secondary textbook boards were also under state supervision. Further, there was a research and publication organization called 'Bangla Academy', which has been believed to be an autonomous body since its establishment. Dhaka University, the nation's largest university, has long been an autonomous body for scholarly print production. It should be noted, however, that the autonomy of Dhaka University was largely meant to be a memorandum on papers and often was violated by the state authority as well as by the administrators inside. This fact has been a common phenomenon in the case of any other university supervised under the 1974 University Ordinance of Bangladesh.[4] Besides these, there were a number of publishers who published classified books – from fiction to scholarly books, from booklets for cooking tips to sports magazines. Currently, the number of publishing houses has increased to a significant degree, though there is hardly any proof of an increase in the number of readers.

While I was doing research for this book, it was crucial to approach the film and music industries. While the former is solely governed by a state office named Film Development Corporation [FDC], whatever that means, the latter is completely a private sector with a huge number of manufacturers. It should be mentioned as relevant information that FDC is also an autonomous body secured by state laws and is supposed to work independently for the development of Bangladeshi films. This, however, is not perceived by the people in general these days. FDC, by and large, has been reduced to a body of officials who are authorized to release, or outlaw, any film for screening publicly and commercially, and in turn, a body that can be manipulated by influential film producers.

When it comes to the enormous influences of the present day's audio-visual production and broadcasting – both in terms of its huge space for propagating specific ideas, and its tremendous capacity to fabricate threads for normative cultural identity – this truly can be identified as an agent of the 'cultural industries' (Hesmondhalgh 2002). Although the current research is not occupied with examining specific products of television, the overall intention of this project is related to the milieu of this medium. After the birth of Bangladesh as an independent nation-state, the sole audio-visual broadcasting agency was Bangladesh Television [BTV]. This was inevitable due to the political circumstances and desire at that time, a nationalized authority that depended thoroughly on the terrestrial broadcasting in regard to the fact that there was no other technological option available. The broadcasting hours ranged from 6 to 8 hours. On some special occasions like *Eid-ul-Fitre* or national elections, special arrangements had been made to transmit programs for longer periods.

---

[4] First organized attempt from the government of independent Bangladesh to ensure what they found both as a demand from the university professionals and students, and an urge from the governmental end as democracy.

Some aspects of this establishment are to be noted since those could be a comprehensible referent to the problem of the research.

It was only during the early '90s that a huge change took place in the field of audio-visual transmission. Not incidentally, it was the same period that ended a long-lasted military dictatorship in Bangladesh, which was marked with some demands for liberalizing the media but achieved nothing special in the course, during and after the first elected BNP government in 1991, except that of the hardware establishment and increase in what is called the entertainment culture. First, there were satellite television channels that became available in 1992 among Bangladeshi viewers – initially mainly for the urban upper middle-class people, and then for the lower middle-class people in the suburbs too.[5] Started under BTV's supervision for news channels like BBC and CNN, soon, it came out of their administration and channels that are categorically known as entertainment ones were broadcast for Bangladeshi viewers. Of course, the process was not a simple or a fast one. There were legal and business arrangements that set the hardware for this new communication system. However, the demand for having access to satellite television channels was pretty high for the affluent families. Then, there was the cable network that made these channels available to a larger audience. It should be made clear that the actualization of the whole process of cable networking was conceived and perceived by the business groups and not by the audience themselves. Paperwork was intense to make an arrangement that was transnational in nature.

What made the scenario distinguished were the obvious changes in the identity of the cultural products. For instance, the channels were either launched from India – like channels of Zee Networks and Sony Entertainment or from Hong Kong like channels from China, Thailand, Hong Kong, and channels of Star Network, or were the typically Western channels that were transmitted from these launching authorities – like HBO, Fox News, English

---

[5] When I mention upper middle-class people, largely I refer to the category of the metropolitan middle class which would be defined next. At the same time on a relational ground it distinguishes itself from the lower or marginal middle class people. As we would discuss later, the vulgar conceptualization of property or asset would not exactly serve to grasp the complexities of the middle class itself. While the middle class is generally being characterized by its salaried nature, education, nuclear family patterns (see Standing 1991, Ahmed and Chowdhury 1997 among others), upper middle class is securing it for generations, staying in Dhaka for at least a generation life time, maintaining an affluent life-style, residing in one of the posh areas of Dhaka and having significant connections both in the native land and overseas. On the other hand, lower or marginal middle-class people are attaining the same virtues of the class, but struggling with under-paid jobs, residing comparatively in the cheaper areas of Dhaka or in the small towns, not having the mobility in a huge scale and so on.

broadcasting through different channels of Star. The point we should note here is that the audience, within a very short period, needed to veer among the imaginary locations, especially with the fact that many 'international' channels experienced a series of shifts in ownership and finally became Indian franchises over the years.

At one point, it was a shock, while at the other point, it appeared to be a doorway to what was already perceived as 'global' or 'cosmopolitan', especially for the middle-class people. Second, initiatives were taken for the private television channels in Bangladesh. More often than not, it was said that the technological advancement that caused these initiatives. Within the next few years, from 1999-2000, there emerged more than five new Bengali medium channels with three Bangladeshi channels among them. The first one was ATN Bangla, then there was *Ekushey* followed by Channel I, Akash Bangla, Tara, and so on. One of the significant features was that the viewership and business initiatives went across the national border – i.e., both from Bangladesh and West Bengal. Except for one, they were all satellite-based. Socially, this fact is crucial. Terrestrial channels could still be reached by more audiences from different social strata. The only channel that was able to broadcast terrestrial codes was banned after some legal battle with the newly elected government.

The audio-visual production and broadcasting remain a complex area to engage. It is interesting to observe that the agencies responsible for establishing television companies were not the same ones interested in Internet ventures. Also, it is not clear what the real conflicts are between those who are launching the television channels and those who are broadcasting the foreign channels. On the contrary, when the government first set rules[6] for a satellite receiver, it instantly then eliminated the probable agencies that could uphold their mission for open information by drafting tough laws. It is also interesting to note that some of these television companies were established in press and news ventures. There are some indications, though very subtle ones, that new forms of alliances and business ties are taking place in contemporary Bangladesh.

---

[6] In this regard, rules and laws are exclusively complicated and ambiguous in Bangladesh. The particular rules for having a private satellite data-receiver, used for internet connection, were drafted on 2000. According to *The Daily Star* feature on 28 December 2004, it was only the previous day, that the government drafted a distinct law for cable television broadcasting and private television – at least 12 years' after the cable television and private channels were on launching. It also reveals that there were no such rules for years. Also, it should be noted that these documents are hardly found in Bangladesh in any comprehensible format. Nor are they easily accessible. Right now, I am designing a research on Bangladeshi media, with special reference to the policy level, which, I hope, would follow my current doctoral research.

Although I tended to distinguish the private sector from the state ones, it has to be mentioned that this has nothing to do, categorically, with what I intend to explore in this research. The facts were meant to indicate, though very crudely, the changes in the background on which the cultural forms – from texts to musical pieces – are generated. Further, the background also reveals the vital threads upon which the public discussions emerge, hence the process of production of discourses.

What matters in fabricating the arguments is the formation of social classes, their specific connection with colonial history – as how it was processual to the specific policies and strategies of the colonial administration, their responses to a particular (cultural) form or genre, their attempt to generate one, their struggle to magnify it and the manifestation of conflicts, if at all. Unlike the stereotypical understanding of social classes, derived from a crude reading of Marxism, classes need examination with a firm understanding of hegemony – the moral, intellectual domination to secure others' consent. One of the major misunderstandings about class formation in the Southern situation, in the subcontinent particularly, revolves around the crude and schematic realization of Marx's thesis of class regardless of one's inclination to Marxism itself. While it is important to comprehend the merits of Marx, the specific features that brought about the formation of nation-states in the subcontinental arena and its subscription to the ability of the salaried class should be taken seriously. Instead of what is identified as the bourgeois class as a product of the industrial base, the Indian subcontinent was presented with the petty-bourgeois salaried class as the ruler.[7] This research, while primarily focusing on understanding the production process of the popular, is likely to be a modest attempt in this regard.

On the one hand, the metropolitan middle class[8] is to be analyzed in my research. On the other hand, the metropolitan poor class[9], as the counterpart of the former and as a hegemonic group, is also a referent in this discussion. Since the very emergence of middle-class domination in Bangladesh has been located long back in the history of colonialism, it is merely a necessary attempt to keep an inner framework consistent with the processes of class formation. It is widely argued and perceived in the academy that the middle class itself is a heterogeneous class. To distinguish different entities of the middle class, scholars often used prior words for adjectional purposes like 'upper', 'lower',

---

[7] Among others, see Standing (1991), Ahmed and Chowdhury (1997), Ahmed (1999).
[8] A term I started using since 1998, first orally and then in the printed materials, to maintain the distinction of its entity. Illustrated partially in Chowdhury (2003).
[9] The reason I do not perceive 'metropolitan poor class' as a generic labor class is definitely its instability in the regulated labor market. Another efficient term could be metropolitan proletariat. But for its assertion as a political entity in Marxian understanding, I avoid it deliberately.

'marginal' etc. By metropolitan middle-class, I mean the particular group of people from the upper-middle-class strata who have been living in the metropolitan for at least a generation, hardly have any plan to move to any other location in Bangladesh, have tremendous mobility beyond the national border, identify themselves to the supposedly cosmopolitan lifestyle and in the linguistic domain, and often have their kin-persons in the diasporic community. On the contrary, by metropolitan poor class, I mean the group of people living in different slums and cheaper places in Dhaka, having tremendous uncertainty about the income source and stability, migrated from the rural or sub-urban locales within one generation or more, hardly have any socio-economic circumstances to return there, often under the threat of eviction by this way or that, identify themselves to the larger section of labor class while lacking the necessary community relationship in an urban society that had been quite important in their past locales of dwelling.

The Concept of Culture Needs to Go Beyond its Generic Meaning

The concept of culture was central, especially considering my background in anthropology, as this is argued as the study of culture since its origin as a separate discipline. The Anglo-Saxon perception of culture revealed an all-encompassing entity of human activities and thoughts, but interestingly rotated within the overarching prejudices about civilization and its interlocutors. Introduced by E. B. Tylor, the definition of culture in anthropological scholarship remained celebrated in academia and has been maintained for a long. The kind of revisions that took place were merely derivative of the original piece. Tylorian definition of culture was so inclusive that no further decisiveness was possible. What, at best, this perception in anthropology served was the 'civilizing mission' as it was propagated and historicized by the Western power. It is interesting to notice that the domination of functionalist tradition in anthropology in the later phase was hardly willing to break through the idealistic nature of the concept. Instead, not only did it further the generic nature, but it also reduced it to some extent to the biological responses and undermined the importance of historicity. At the onset of dominant functionalist research in anthropology, and generally in social science, contesting the existing concept of culture seemed tough, though necessary (early anthropological concepts were discussed in detail in Ahmed and Chowdhury 2003).

Asad and Dixon (1985) and later Asad (1988) understood culture as a representational system. This concept helps us a lot not only to comprehend cultural process as a set of activities and ideas, but also the particular ways that make those imperative to its subjects. Thus, it opens up the possibility of identifying the questions of authority and subjection in the above process (Asad discussed in Ahmed and Chowdhury 1997).

Gramsci's notion of popular culture and his search for a 'National-Popular'

The research is grounded upon the onset of polemics and debates on popular. In regard to the impacts Gramscian understanding of popular culture caused on social research, Gramsci demands proper attention in many ways. Firstly, it is Gramsci (trans. 1973) who underlined the importance of the concept in the course of social investigation. Secondly, Gramsci critically examines the interrelation of the concept with social classes and also with hegemony, a concept explored and has made a very significant contribution in the course of social scientific investigations over time. Thirdly, researches that were either on popular culture, or on people's political process, consequently, engaged with Gramsci's arguments in this regard.

The work by Forgacs (1999) on Gramsci claimed to be monumental not only because it compiled the best of his notebooks (trans. 1973) but also because it proposed a precise reading to those. Referring to the then-Italian situation, Gramsci's search was for a popular culture that could tend towards forming what he urged for as 'national-popular.' For Gramsci, it was the networking between the national intellectuals and the mass people that could lead to the necessary revolutionary changes in society (Gramsci 1973). I doubt the possibility of setting apart the conceptual tools from the specific political mission that had been crucial for the Gramscian way of Marxist politics. I propose this in the context of the charge against some postcolonial thinkers for doing the same. Regarding the specific goal of this research, however, engaging with Gramsci is utmost necessary. His understanding can provide us with certain guidelines about how these ideas could best be used to understand a different location, yet in a different temporal condition – contemporary Bangladesh. The reason Gramsci's propositions are so crucial is his merits in investing the class structures, their relation to the specific popular cultures and the potential force for changing its course. However, it is important to note that Forgacs warns us about the particular Italian situation of the 30s. The transition towards modernity, unlike the counterparts in Europe like Britain, France, or even Germany, was phenomenal to Italy at that time.

> The cultural situation in which Gramsci was writing was one of transition to modernity, and this needs to be taken into account when reading these notes. At the time of his imprisonment a large market for books had not developed in Italy, mainly because of a still high illiteracy rate, though illustrated magazines and comics were taking off. Cinema and sound-recording had been around since the turn of the century, but radio broadcasting was still in its infancy and television would not be introduced until the 1950s. (Forgacs 1999, 363).

What makes Gramsci's position fascinating for the Bangladeshi situation is its pointed engagement with the synthetic nature of Italian culture or, for instance, what Gramsci intended to conceive as popular culture contrary to bourgeois or elite culture. Even after 70 years of his time, and yet after so many events that took place in global history, his arguments claim to be relevant in contemporary Bangladesh. For example, as will be revealed in the coming chapter, the role of foreign products in shaping the popular culture in Bangladesh appears to be comparable to what Gramsci found in Italy. It needs to be clear that, although the journey towards it appears to be an endless one, especially in Southern societies like Bangladesh, certain elements of modernity are to be imported on the backdrop of an efficient modern nation-state. As referred to in the background, a comparable kind of atmosphere was ensured in Bangladesh only in the last two decades. Therefore, the transformational phase in Bangladesh, or I would like to contend, in any society from the South, appears to be comparable.

But it is not the probable comparison on an empirical level that underscores the significance of Gramsci, but rather the dialectical vision of culture that he maintained. This is where, probably, Gramsci has been taken so seriously in contemporary academia in a range of disciplines of humanities and social sciences. He never was skeptical about the possibility of the subaltern cultural forms being incorporated into the dominant culture, or about the possibility of subaltern people being recipients of the dominant culture. This, I argue, should be underlined in its specific reference to Bangladesh. While I analyze the readership or viewership of the contemporary film genres among the people from the poor class, or responses by the marginal people towards the importance of the propagated international education, the resemblance is obvious.

Still, I suppose there are two specific consciousnesses needed for borrowing Gramsci's framework into the location and temporality of this project entails with. One is about the lack of awareness of the probable processes of manufacturing the popular, while the other is about Gramsci's overemphasis on the written forms of culture. To put it straight, I would like to argue that those two are inseparable and it is where Stuart Hall seems to be more relevant in this project. Understandably, Gramsci was considering a completely different state mechanism both under fascism and without the modern vibration of communication system, more importantly in the absence of the state's usage of mass media for manifesting its facets. This is exactly where the modern nation-states and their allies are working. Until the post-World War II situation, the European state machinery did not discover the strategies of mass media. Or put it in specific locations, this is what was identified by Hall in Britain, and arguably a case of Bangladesh too. Further, with special reference to the theories on discourse and representation, the concept of textuality went beyond its apparent meaning and revealed a set of ideas and values that set the condition for the production of knowledge (see Foucault 1989 [1972]). The historical condition that was Gramsci's concern provided hardly any space for the extra-print media for knowledge production. On the contrary, the huge space that is being celebrated in modern nation-states is that of newly emerged media that work on specific discursive fields. This field, I would like to maintain, is an extensive elaboration of textuality that surpasses obvious printable preconditions, rather inscribed in the modern psyche.

Folk-urban drift, popular, power-bloc and manipulation

Stuart Hall (1965, 1981, and 1988) is one of the few scholars who maintained for a long time to further Gramsci's arguments. While Gramsci saw popular culture as opposed to the elite culture and, at the same time, as a potential foundation for revolutionary changes, Hall fundamentally subscribes to the view. Further, he remains critical of the distinction between, and relationship among, the popular and the power-blocs. This awareness gives us a chance to investigate the complexities of a hegemonic structure and the possibilities for a 'popular' to turn into a 'power-bloc' as such. Founded upon Gramsci's ideas of 'organic', Hall's (1988) critical vision, for instance, examines the popularity of 'Thatcherian doctrine' in the then British society. His fascinating findings show us the influence that the Thatcher government managed to generate among the British population in general and the labor class in particular. This influence, as argued, was an outcome of the deliberate attempt to address political aspects with the moral and theological aspects. Hall's work on 'Thatcherian doctrine' was at odds with what he proposed on power-bloc (1981). But with further investigation, we can be sure that his thesis as to be a cutting-edge extension of the former one. Another aspect of Hall's intervening thesis that appears to be crucial is the drift between folk culture and what he had explored in the metropolitan locales (1965).

> This folk culture was a part of communal ways of life or 'organic' communities ... Folk art survived the coming of the cities – though not ... without loss of quality. There was certainly a vigorous urban and early industrial 'folk' culture. Gradually, however, much of it has disappeared with the development of industrialization, as the close communities have been dispersed and the rhythms of work have been altered by the development of technology and the machine ... Since the folk culture and the way of life were so nearly interchangeable, we cannot now wish to revive the culture without restoring the way of life. The desire to return to the organic community is a cultural nostalgia which only those who did not experience the cramping and inhuman conditions of that life can seriously indulge. (Hall and Whannel 1965, 52-3).

One can easily notice the level of engagement with historicity that Hall (with Whannel) has shown here. The dislocation and disruption of the folk, which were obvious in the process of industrialization, were central to his engagement with the issue. It is very exciting to notice Hall's attentiveness in marking the cultural production in a given condition even long back in his early career. This carefulness would again be evident in the coming extraction. Before that, I would like to engage with the positions Appadurai and Fiske uphold. Though differently, both denied associating with the Hall's position this way or that. Appadurai, as we would see next, emphasized the nature of the cross-strata of contemporary cultural production. I am very concerned with the specificity of the visual products in and from the present day's Indian industry with its special reference to the emerging diasporic audience, and I found Appadurai's contention a very interesting one. While it has its merit, especially what he finds in the very condition of cultural production in contemporary Indian films, one should not ignore the ahistorical nature of its claim. Hall's cautious attitude towards the manipulation, of the mass media in this case, is precisely formulated in his profound understanding of 'corruption': "…typical 'art' of the mass media today is not a continuity from, but a *corruption of,* popular art." (Hall and Whannel 1965, 68, emphasis original).

It must be noticed that Hall never confuses folk with the popular, rather characterizes the painful transformation and distinguishes in terms of what he named as 'intention' and 'typical offerings.' The question of transformation, I suppose, is crucial in the modern setting of cultural production. Consistent scrutiny from the researchers' point of view needs to be assured. We can find a comparable, if not trickier, in the reinvention of folk in the audio-visual industry of Bangladesh. It is specifically complicated by the fact that a number of typically defined 'rural' and 'traditional' singers are sharing the space in audio production with a number of urban singers who promote a genre called fusion, a kind of reproduction of the orthodox folk songs, could best be defined as 'corruption' as it was named by Hall. What is important here is that these two groups of performers are not in any comparable social status. Further, this particular process of production is capable enough to mess up to define, or even to perceive, any comprehensive boundary on a certain point (discussed in Chowdhury 2000, 2001a). At this point, what Hall identified as popular in Britain, cannot be traced in a typical Southern society like Bangladesh, established on the remains of a colonial history, or in a different temporal condition.

However, Hall himself found difficulties in the manufacturing terrain of cultural codes. And this was not by the mass media as such, but by the state authority using the media space (Hall et al. 1978). After consistent investigation of the British popular culture, or the wave that came out in Europe, for more than twenty years, Hall found the penetrative role of the then-Thatcher administration in both manufacturing and shaping the popular. He was spot on analyzing it as a deliberate attempt to deactivate the poles of cultural politics and was understandably cited by several scholars of the later age, including Sparks (1992) and Fiske (1992), in their stimulating pieces on popular culture and journalism. Since Hall is believed to be one with the foundational knowledge in the genre of popular culture, he has been under serious discussions and polemics. While Hall remains central for understanding complex, and often obvious, relationships between 'popular' and 'power-bloc', it is interesting and confusing to note that Gramsci, comparatively, has not been engaged that much. Apparently, Gramsci's formulation reads against what Hall suggests. For me, Gramsci provided the impetus of reading the extensive cultural field, and Hall's is an intriguing extension of the former where he warns us not to perceive the binary as 'class-against-class' (Hall 1981, 238).

Denial to accept popular in relation to class

John Fiske, on the other hand, denies any essential meaning of the popular. To put it in other words, Fiske is skeptical about associating popularity with the formation of social classes. Rather his is the position to cancel out any possibility of having an objective basis for popular culture. Given the specific feeling and sense of collectivity people show at a particular moment, as he puts it, Fiske goes for the subjective conditions that formulate the perception of a popular. According to him, 'the people' cannot be identified or designed as a research population for empirical study as it does not provide any objective condition. He used three parallel terms to locate the 'popular' – the people, the popular, the popular – and find them having fluid attributes and, thus, are bound to a particular social category. By 'the people', he means "this shifting set of social allegiances, which are described better in terms of people's felt collectivity than in terms of external sociological factors such as class, gender, age, race, region, or what have you." (Fiske 1989a, 24)

The fluid nature of the people is what is marked in Fiske's position. Interestingly enough, Hall never asserts any essential meaning of the popular, or for instance, of the people. Instead, he in turn became much more receptive to the changes that had taken place in the mighty cultural industry and was sensitive about using the very concept he had been engaged in for so long – the 'popular.' Long before the specific project of examining the Thatcher regime, he went on to analyze how the concept was becoming problematic. In response to the pronunciation of Mrs. Thatcher 'We have to limit the power of the trade unions because that is what the people want', Hall concludes that "there is no fixed content to the category of 'popular culture', so there is no fixed subject to attach to it – 'the people' (Hall 1981, 239). In the course of making an attempt to relate pleasure and commodity with the popular – a category that he finds as 'shifting sets of allegiances that cross all social categories' – Fiske, to me, appears to be tautological. What I find most disturbing is his usage of a phrase like 'social experience' (Fiske 1989b, 24). As I like to argue, if it is to be experienced, there must be a traceable line between the experienced ones and the inexperienced – hence, a loose form of social class. Further, my point is that

Introduction

if there is a significant transgression of this line by the respective people from different what he names as 'social categories', then there is a strong possibility of the existence of manipulative structures that can simulate some kind of feelings even to the inexperienced ones. And this stimulation is powerful enough to mesmerize a group of people. Here comes the significance of the production of cultures and discourses.

Introducing 'Public Culture' to discuss cosmopolitan production

While Gramsci and Hall are considered to be the foremost theoreticians for the conceptual foundation of the current research, Arjuna Appadurai (1988), among others, needs to get proper attention in the conceptualization of popular. He straightforwardly argues about what he finds as inadequate in the dichotomy of popular vs. elite. In this line, he upholds the concept of 'public culture'. According to him, this concept is capable of going beyond the boundary set by the dichotomy and is necessary for understanding contemporary cultural production, especially in the subcontinental preconditions. Distinctiveness of Appadurai's position is seen when, after quite a long period in terms of contemporary scholarly production, Dwyer and Pinney (2001) go along with the argument as a framework for their remarkable anthology on visual cultural production. Appadurai (with Breckenridge) explains their concern over the conceptual limitations that they found in popular culture:

> Part of our long-term concern is to persuade both historians and anthropologists that current notions of popular, folk or traditional cultural forms simply are not adequate for the interpretative challenges posed by the cosmopolitan forms of today's public cultures. Where popular culture is often the product of urban, commercial and state interests, where folk culture is often a response to the competitive cultural policies of today's nation-states, and where traditional culture is often the result of conscious deliberation or elaboration, these terms clearly need rethinking. We intend that our argument in favor of the rubric of public culture provide a fruitful vantage point for such consideration. (Appadurai and Breckenridge 1988, 8-9, emphasis original).

I have chosen a relatively longer quotation, considering my usual benchmark, as it concisely summarizes where Appadurai (and his allies) are coming from. He maintained his position even when he tended to scrutinize globalization in the later phase (see Appadurai 1990 and 1996). It is exciting to observe, and helpful to engage with, that they have unmasked the modern processes of cultural production in every possible form – folk, popular, traditional. That they noticed the obvious responsive character of these forms towards the massive structure, for instance, the state-machine itself, is of great significance. But, at the same time, it is interesting to notice them to be deliberately unwilling to engage with that massive structure. While I am much aware of what is deserved by this thesis, especially in probing the Indian cultural production, truly on a global scale these days, I like to remain skeptical about the kind of conceptual frameworks being suggested by the diasporic postcolonial theorists from India. I firmly believe that the fact is an outcome of the influential Indian scholarship around the Western academia – with their glorification of the postcolonial Indian substances onto a global scale, a necessary attribute for the sake of constructing India not as a hegemonic structure by itself, but as an antagonistic one to the global cultural products. However, this is not my rightmost priority at this moment, but it will be one in my lifetime if we have a reconfigured and extended debate on 'popular' culture and its 'global' manifestation. However, with the advent of the ever-expanding culture industry and renewed meanings of 'nation' in a particular geography-bound space and at a juncture, the debate is likely to take a different route. The following quotation would be an interesting testimony to his (their) proposition. It is interesting to notice two particular words there – 'escape' and 'cosmopolitanism'. These are exactly where I like to refer to what I have mentioned as ahistorical and what I cautiously propose as a celebration of the Indian diaspora.

> Why use the adjective *public* for cultural forms that appear to be well described by so many other, more familiar ones like popular, mass, folk, consumer, national, or middle class? The term *public* is not a neutral or arbitrary substitute for all these existing alternatives. Nevertheless, it appears to be less embedded in such highly specific Western dichotomies and debates as high versus low culture; mass versus elite culture; and popular or folk versus classical culture. With the term *public culture* we wish to escape these by now conventional hierarchies and generate an approach which is open to the cultural nuances of cosmopolitanism and of the modern in India. (Appadurai and Breckenridge 1988, 6, emphasis original).

Asad's concept of 'Core Values' and Western Cultural Hegemony

Despite his significant contribution to understanding anthropology as a discipline – i.e., his vision of what he names as the anthropology of the western cultural hegemony, and in the study of religion and modernity, Asad, in this work, is engaged directly in a very limited way. His understanding of 'core values' (Asad 1993) in class formation is at the heart of the conceptualization of my work. That is, on a particular trajectory, the class – middle class in particular and in the British context in his work – upholds some 'core values'. These are the attributes that must be noticed and analyzed in detail for a proper understanding of the class and its actions and agency at that particular moment. With special reference to the hype of the Rushdie affair in the then British society, the

Introduction 15

reactions and activities generated among the commoners were, he maintained, to conform and secure the proper British identity (Asad 1993). This was the expectation, so bluntly expressed, from the state's point of view, whereas this was exactly how the middle-class population was acting accordingly. No matter whatever threats were given to Rushdie, it was then the impulse to reshape the British Muslim population into a desired direction, towards where the state could find them properly governed. The intelligentsia and educated people, according to him, did not put any impediment to this desire for governance; rather enhanced the authority and secured their agency in a post-colonial setup where a huge population came from the colonies themselves.

I considered that engaging very thoroughly with Asad was never at the scope of my research, precisely because of the fact that it would take a complete body of work, but at the same time, his theses are at the foundation of my route of investigation. He maintains his position by consistently insisting on the task of anthropologists to look for the hegemony of the Western culture.[10] It helps us out explaining the contemporary cultural production around the globe, and its shared meaning across the national boundaries. It provides us with the understanding that we can unpack the cultural reality not only by referring to its forms but also to the historical structures upon which these forms are being generated.

---

[10] This remains, as mentioned earlier, a consistent position in Asad. Moreover, this position gets sharper day by day as he proceeds on to new scholarly projects. He is, I firmly believe, among those very few scholars in the present globe, who never gets in a position where contradicting their own previous ideas appears to be a way out. For the concept of 'anthropology of western cultural hegemony', among other pieces, see Asad's work in 1988.

Chapter 2

The Zia Manifestation

The regime (roughly from 1977 to 1981) ruled by the military dictator turned into political icon Major General Ziaur Rahman should be treated as a crucial phase in understanding contemporary Bangladesh. It has certain political merits of its own and is actually a subject of much discussion both in Bangladesh and beyond. The rise of Ziaur Rahman and, consequently, the formation of BNP [Bangladesh Nationalist Party] has long been a crucial issue in the Bangladeshi political process, of course in the defined terrains of prejudices. With very few exceptions, either they fall into the kind of propagandist pamphlets or the kind demonizing him without critical arguments and largely on emotional grounds. This particular tendency seems to have a connection with the bloody political history of Bangladesh.

Before the War of Independence in 1971, Zia was a Major in the Bengal Regiment, a sect under the Pakistani military. Eventually, regarding his pro-Bangladesh role in the war of independence (Muktijuddho), he became one of the many officers in the independent Bangladesh. His role and influence in Bangladeshi politics and power nexus, however, was changed drastically after the assassination of Sheikh Mujibur Rahman on August 15, 1975. Mujib, the nationalist leader of the freedom movement of Bangladesh, and his party, Awami League, formed the first parliamentary government after independence. Within a few years, he had to face serious trouble both at domestic and international levels. While he was challenged by the US for his overt position in the then Non-Alliance Movement [NAM] and pro-USSR bloc, he was further troubled both by the radical left groups and the extreme right groups at home. He eventually banned most of the political parties in Bangladesh and switched to a one-party presidential form in 1974 that included some other ally political parties. This only worsened his position. Finally, he was assassinated by a military coup. Comparable to the previous phase ruled by Mujib, the next few months claim to be the most incomprehensible phase of Bangladeshi history. Mujib's assassination was followed by a series of military coups and counter-coups, and those events took place only within a few weeks. Zia came into power on

November 7, 1975, through a 'popular sepoy revolution'[1], as has been claimed by many of the pro-BNP and pro-military analysts.

However, the uprising of the lower-ranked army against Mujib should be seen as a more complicated event than it appears to be in the regular history books. Zia, after securing his power, went on to establish a political facet of his power. The crucial point was that of accessing support from different interest groups – both in the army and the political parties. BNP was announced as a political party on September 1, 1978, and has remained an important political entity till now.

Apart from the mainstream political implications of General Zia's regime, along with its remains, I intend to explore its cultural meaning. While I intend to do so, I am fully aware of the risk of separating political from cultural, which, in turn, seems to be absurd. The thin line between political and cultural is more and more being seen as blurred in contemporary academia. Yet, what I mean to do is a schematic reading of the potential consequences of the Zia regime in the public life or consciousness, beyond the typically defined political arena. In this line, the task is not to separate the cultural from the political, instead of distinguishing a set of attributes that could largely be located in the socio-cultural life. In the end, my intention is to identify the representational rules that had been crucial at a certain phase of Bangladesh, as I like to contend, to advocate certain kinds of codes. To make my point more focused, my purpose is to pose the argument that the Zia doctrine became popular not by chance but rather by an engineered project. Further, this project of popularizing had certain purposes as well as technologies to enhance it.

Understanding of Zia Regime

The fundamental encouragement came from Stuart Hall's work on Thatcherism in Great Britain (Hall 1981). Hall's main argument was about how, despite its fascistic nature, the Thatcher doctrine came out as a populist trend during the 80s. By thoroughly examining what he defined as Thatcherite manifestation, Hall pointed out some specific projects that were deliberately executed to comply with the values and desires of the working-class people. Considering the huge popularity Zia was able to generate, it is interesting to analyze the inner tactics of this popularity – a discursive practice that is fundamental for what is being named democratic politics. My modest attempt is to underline the constructing strategies applied by the Zia regime, not only for pampering an identity that had long been fractional but also the attempt to iconize it as deep-rooted referents.

---

[1] For example, see Hossain (1988). This kind of representation of both Zia and the 'revolution' is to be examined critically. The course of Bangladeshi military, as it were, has never been under critical study. At the same time, the pro-Zia forces in Bangladesh are able to assert the meanings to the events they find significant.

This is not to say that the regime had started as something out of the blue. Image construction of the leader has always been a crucial strategy in modern nation-states. It should be noted that the former populist leader in Bangladesh – Sheikh Mujibur Rahman – was also illustrated extensively by the state machine. Where the Zia regime succeeded disproportionately was in maintaining a systematic iconization of some eccentric images and actions. It appeared so strong that even after a very short-lived regime, Zia himself remained a huge influence as a political icon. The framework, derived from the contribution by Hall, is to identify some basic ideas that had been propagated loudly under deliberate supervision by Zia and the state organs. Then, it is to explore the nature of how Zia was portrayed – both in the pictorial form and the textual form. I contend that the mentioned ideas and the portrayal of his image cannot be separated. In other words, the image of Zia is integral to the propagated ideas.

It would be relevant to engage with the question of why Zia's popularity is a probing theme. Unlike its former counterparts, it never had taken popularity for granted but considered popularity as a project of implanting images, nurturing it to its next phase, backing it up with adequate words and finally broadcasting it with sheer speed and intensity. In this line, the regime invokes a denial of popularity as a direct correlation with the people as a generic entity. It does not claim popularity, but cultivates it. This is where the quest is so important. Especially when we are to explore the popularizing projects in contemporary Bangladesh, the Zia regime can well be the foremost reference of all.

On a general understanding, the political analyses in Bangladesh considered the processes of the Zia regime in a concerted manner. What Zia had been perceived as the chief architect, both by the supporters and the antagonists, is that of Bangladeshi identity. This must be understood as a continuation of contestation in the process of nationalism, nation-building and national identity formation, which started long back in the colonial period. Still, the political analyses at best reduced the Zia regime to be an Islamizing process. This is not to say here that the Zia regime should not be characterized for its tendency towards Islamic motifs and codes. But a mere term of 'Islamization', I argue, is not capable of grasping the level of intensity and complexity of the processes that took place in a certain period, not even is it able to contest the essential assertion of seeing Islam as a potential resource of what is being propagated as 'fundamentalism'.

For Zia, Islam had never been an overt justification for the legal and moral restructuring of Bangladeshi society, which was the case in Pakistan during the same period with General Ziaul Huq as the military dictator (Talbot 1998). More importantly, his overt affiliation with Islamic codes was surpassed by his covert relationship with the global superpower and its cultural manifestation. This is the reason why it cannot be convincingly defined as Islamization. What made the issue more complicated was the assassination of Zia within a very short period. More often, the assassination acts as a crucial testament to his image – for what the regime is being argued here as a machinery for deliberate construction. Subsequently, what I mean by Zia Manifestation should never be seen within a tight time frame of his life. Instead, it should be seen as a style of representation – rotated around his image, which has an extended influence till the present – which is exercised repetitively and for specific purposes. Further, the strategies of this image construction have long been appropriated for implanting second-generation icons. This is a fact that should be understood regarding the activities in contemporary Bangladesh.

Instead of being trapped in a superficial understanding, Zia could captivatingly be perceived in a schematic way. As mentioned earlier, my intention is solely concerned with the cultural aspect of the construction, and not a political or historical analysis whatsoever.

Three Pillars of Zia Manifestation

As I have mentioned earlier, my intention is not to illustrate a historical narration of the matter, but instead to explore what I pathologically term as cultural meaning of Zia manifestation. Accordingly, I would like to underline three basic constructional features of Zia manifestation that were crucial for the popularizing mission. Those are a) the construction of India as the most harmful enemy of the Bangladeshi 'self'; b) the construction of America as the most imaginable locale for a desirable lifestyle; c) the construction of the military as the image of bravery and power. To avoid confusion, my point is not to perceive these features as appropriations of the already popular codes at the time. Nor do I substantially see them as merely the reasons for maintaining popularity on a certain point. Instead, I would like to argue them as the expressions of some conscientiously nurtured phenomena that had specific potentials.

Construction of India as the most harmful enemy of the Bangladeshi 'self'

The architects of the post-colonial subcontinental cartography have had their sheer impacts over the decades. This fact should be seen in the enormous pain of dislocation, despair, deprivation, and distrust. Regardless of the actual number of migrants from India, their presence in the newly independent nation-state since 1947 played another crucial part. Above all, the emergence of India as a dominant state helped the mission for which Zia supposedly can easily be identified in the first place. In this line, Zia at best corresponded to a remote feeling that almost lost its relevance since the Pakistani rulers appeared as the immediate enemy within a very short period of the emergence of Pakistan in 1947. Only an independent Bangladesh was the right space to nurture the feeling that had been so strong during the laborious partition of British India.

It is important to note that Zia is much referred to what is being named as 'Islamizing', especially by the defined secularist camp. Keeping in mind the central mission of identity building, Zia's dealing with Islam can best be perceived as a component of anti-India manifestation and a deliberate reference to the logic of the 'two-nation theory'[22]. In this line, we can tentatively perceive the accusation of making Bangladesh a Pakistan, made by the pro-Awami League and anti-Zia people, also on a cultural ground. My intention here is not to reduce the significance or danger of his mission but rather to explore the cultural meaning of this accusation.

Construction of America as the most imaginable locale for a desirable lifestyle

The rebuilding of the American image in the public psyche should be considered a crucial feature of the Zia regime. Regarding the US's role as the opposition during the war of independence in Bangladesh, it became one of the most hated entities in the independent Bangladesh. Although this statement claims to portray a clear picture without any grey area in it, the actual situation of course was much contested in nature. Politically speaking, the post-independent Bangladesh, right from the beginning, had an interesting undercurrent power network with several pro-American pockets – both in the military establishment and in the civil institutions, a fact that gradually became apparent in the later phase. In the military, the pocket contained groups like the loyal ones to former Pakistani military authority or the groups tentatively accused of the assassination of Mujib. On the other hand, a number of public intellectuals like poets, columnists, journalists, and professors maintained a pro-American stance in civil institutions – a fact that is revealed more in the later phases in Bangladesh. Considering partisan works from both ends – i.e., from the Awami League point of view (Mukul 1982, for example) and the BNP point of view (Hossain 1984, for example), the significance of this faction in the history of Bangladesh can be perceived. Yet, while I assert the fact of the construction of America in the Zia manifestation, I mean mainly a cultural act in its generic meaning. One must be aware of the distinction between American influence over different power pools at a certain point and its acknowledgment of a desirable lifestyle overtly. The latter cannot be seen, I would like to argue, entirely as a political process, nor merely a result of policy shift.

---

[2] 'Two-nation' theory is referred to in the proposal made by the Muslim League leader Mohammad Ali Zinnah to his British counterpart and eventually was carried out as to be a solution of the question of national identity after the British India. On the basis of religious identity, the idea was to create two different nations after the British rule in what was called the Indian subcontinent.

What made the transformation more significant was its reduction of America, far from all it did during the war in 1971 and in the post-independence phase, to a prosperous land. It is not possible to correlate with the everyday consumption of American goods – foods, clothes, home apparel, or electronics – for it had never been the case in Bangladesh. Instead, until very recently, roughly from the mid-90s, consuming American goods in Bangladesh had always been tough compared to some other nationals like India or China. In this line, the tendency had very little to do with the tangible America, but with what America could probably mean culturally. And then the meaning had no fixed arena of corresponding; instead was a continuous process of construction.

Some of the contemporary analysts counted Zia for what they thought of as an avenue towards modernity in Bangladesh. Some features could be mentioned in the same line of assertion. It is also apparent in the ventures of the Zia regime that it deliberately used emerging development discourses and referred to what can be termed *developmental consciousness*. Considering its constructional endeavors and capability, I would rather be interested in perceiving the Zia phase as a manipulative strategy towards modernity. The obvious provocation of analyzing the Zia regime as a voyage towards modernity comes from the similar events I have considered here, especially his overt association with the idea of 'youth', let alone his deliberate attempts to include a large number of meritorious students in BNP politics. At the same time, the perils of doing so remain. First, it leaves us in a place of uncritically subscribing to the concept of modernity and positing it on a comparative scale. Second, it conceals the possibility of critically looking at Zia's attempts to legitimize his regime on a global stage. We should be aware of the sheer influence of the discourses of modernity during the late 70s.

Construction of the military as the image of bravery and power

Among the three pillars, the last one may be considered the most significant. This claim has particular reference to the antipathy towards the Pakistani rulers during the last two decades before independence. Militarism had been a consistent point of criticism and dissatisfaction from the Bangladeshi point of view. Pakistan was perceived as a military state by the commoners. The sensation only furthered with the unprecedented experience of loss and suffering caused by the Pakistani military. The emergence of Bangladesh as an independent state in 1971 could somehow renovate the idea of a state, understandably on a liberal ground. This is what the agenda of the Mujib regime was (1971-1975) too.

A blueprint regarding the military establishment can subtly be felt in the Zia regime. The main thesis was to assert such an image of the military that could be accepted by a significant portion of the 'people'. Further, it went on to regenerate a relishing illustration of the army that led to a middle-class desire to take part in the military. One can argue that the military rule needed its subjects to accept its appearance, and Zia tried to build that trust in the military. While I have no such opposition to this claim, I am very interested in taking account of this transformation in the cultural sphere of everyday life, especially that of the middle class. Without much exception, the educated middle class dreamt of sending their boys to the military. Military recruiting tests appeared in the national dailies with straight claims and bold outlooks. The construction process had, therefore, a clear reciprocal aspect.

Image of Zia and Replication

Zia's image must be seen on the backdrop of the pillars mentioned above. The image has further been deployed by some agencies with a conscious mission of iconizing, thus popularizing, it. Although the remark could be felt as a speculative one, one can look into the meanings of the production of a series of images and conclude the conscious nature of the process. Many tactics seemed to be copied in the later phase – first by Ershad[3] and then by Tarek Zia[4], eldest son of Zia. The striking aspect of Zia's image was that it never appeared to be discontinuous in its forms of production. I mean to say that the visual representations of Zia and the textual construction of the same person delicately corresponded with each other. For example, as he had been constructed as a 'brave soldier' in the texts – in leaflets, pamphlets, and in the commissioned scholarly works, it would also be backed up by a poster with his photo in army costume, taken from a lower angle, attending an army parade, and receiving salute. Another example, quite an interesting one, could be taken from the much-debated matter of the 'Declaration of Independence.' BNP keeps on claiming that it was Zia who, after the Pakistani army attacked on March 25,

---

[3] Lt. General Hossain Mohammad Ershad. He became the military ruler in 1981, after some months of Zia's assassination. Unlike some other military juntas, he captured power with some clever moves. He did not seize power just after Zia's killing, rather, as the army chief, expressed army support to BNP and continued his support until the next president, Mr. Abdus Sattar, a veteran BNP leader, was elected. It was only then he decided to declare military rule and eventually staged some tribunals for what he declared as for justice of Zia's assassination. He remained in the power, first as the military dictator, and then with electoral sanitization, until he was overthrown by what is named as a popular uprising in 1990.

[4] Tareq Zia is currently (2002 onwards) the senior sectary general of ruling BNP. He is said to be one of the tycoons in the business world of Bangladesh and with having strong holds in the underworld world. This is something that remains in the public discussion and at the same time, remains under veil as no such study is available – neither in scholarly form nor in journalistic one. Some glimpses on his capability would be illustrated in chapter five.

1971, declared independence of Bangladesh from a remote radio station. The claim necessarily cancels out the charismatic leadership of Mujib and his call for freedom. After being elected in the first parliamentary election after the Ershad regime, the BNP circulated a poster with Zia's photo reading a paper in a studio that could remind one of a radio station. The poster also had some text message: "the declarer of our independence, take our salute," Amazingly, the costume of Zia was that of the Bangladeshi army, and not what the Bengal Regiment had to put on. This is where my argument seems to be compelling. Far from being 'real' or 'true', the process of representation should mean creating certain spaces and readings in a particular context.

With a close examination of Zia's image, we can trace the 'try and error' methods that took place in the course of constructing a hero in the public sphere. From a stubborn and ambitious military officer to a smart negotiator with the foreign counterparts, or from an anti-India campaigner to an Americanized youth – Zia was a series of referents in his political career from 1977 to 1981. No matter if these facts had anything to do with the actual situations, the entire manufacturing machine went on portraying these facts with specific care and attention. At the time of Mujib's assassination in 1975, Zia must have been somewhere very close to the top of the state machine. But the fact that he remained invisible till there was a sudden coup in the military that eliminated all his probable rivals within and beyond the military could be read as a crucial testimony of the image construction we are talking about. For the regime, Zia was far from a leader to cash on people's support, but rather an icon to implant in the public psyche. This could be the reason why Zia, as an icon, sustained long after he was killed.

The foremost strategy for implanting Zia's image and popularizing it was the deliberate use of pictorial images along with words about him. Never did the process try to conceal the arrogance of Zia. Instead, the visual representation of Zia seemed to have the defined mission of depicting him as an arrogant military officer – with his eyes covered under Ray-Ban glasses, the army uniform, with his stand-alone posture taken by a tilted-up camera. On another occasion where he was supposed to take part in development activities – like digging canals for irrigation, a twisting project discovered by his regime – with jeans, a golf cap, and still the Ray-Ban covering his eyes, Zia was digging canals by his hand, or taking a rest beside some paddy field. The pictorial images were transmitted all over Bangladesh – through printed posters or wall paintings by some local artists.

The craft of depicting an autocratic military ruler as a 'public figure' kept on succeeding in the contemporary Bangladesh. At some point, this is not Zia who is being replicated but the architectural principles that are being used and reused for implanting a 'popular'.

Chapter 3

Nation as a Mode of Consumption

Legacy of a Dichotomy

This chapter seeks to explore the nature of consumerism in contemporary Bangladesh and, consequently, its significance in organizing the meanings of what is being propagated as a national identity at a particular moment. Nowadays, it is being urged by a number of scholars (among others, Anderson 1983; Hall 1991) that identity is a discursive phenomenon. My attempt is solely as a subscriber to that view. In this line, I do not intend to examine and place the 'authentic' Bangladeshi national culture, nor do I stand for identifying the phenomena that supposedly validate this 'authentic'. Instead, what I anticipate to inquire about is the process of authentication and its relevance to the mentioned consumerism. Having been aware of the significance of the history of identity formation, I should also make it clear that the process of national identity formation in Bangladesh is somewhat not the main focus of this search. In brief, the focuses are a) how the nation repeatedly refers to the availability, or for instance, supply, of new consumer goods and b) how the consumption itself, of course by the well-off social class people, or the desire-to-consume is underlining the very representation of the nation. In doing so, I think it would be relevant to take a brief account of the schematic framework of anthropological knowledge deployed to approach economic activities.

Though old-fashioned and cliche' in nature, the very debate on consumption is still common in the orthodoxy of social scientific literature (Carrier 1996, for example). That is about the inclination of the concept – whether it is an economic category or a cultural one. Especially in the anthropological literature (Spencer 1996, for example), the anticipation of this concept, as a viable category too, seems to have a connection with the long-established and painfully asserted schema of the formalism-substantive binary. It is commonsensical to perceive why the anthropologists felt it necessary to study the economic nature of certain human groups, not to mention those of the 'simple' ones, but at the same time, it is too difficult to comprehend why they had chosen to befit themselves in the terrain of economics – both as a set of defined categories and concepts, and as a discipline of approaching what it presupposed as obvious. I am aware of while claiming the falsity of the binary, the differences between the two positions and find no point in beginning with the differences they have. Considering the foundational principles of the discipline, as it had been said so far, it could have been more sensible to have an approach to the writing culture.

Surprisingly it did not happen in the course of the anthropological scholarship. However, the latter surely can claim special attention to its credit in this line.[1]

While the binary has long been cherished in the specific discipline of anthropology to provide an understanding of the economic activities in *certain* societies as such in the direction of this way or that (for example, Leclair and Schneider 1968; Polyani 1958), it has greatly reduced, at the same time, the possibility of exploring the issue to a further level. This is especially true if we consider the complex nature of the contemporary economy on presumably a global stage and within national boundaries. However, the apparent meaning of these observations should not be left out in this way without further grounding it into the urge that the early anthropologists have in their investigations. By and large, the formalists contested the very assumption of the economists that the 'simple' societies had no relevance with the principle of economics (for example, Burling 1962; Sahlins 1972). In this line, their ventures even realized the necessity of comprehending those societies according to the framework applicable on a global scale.

Concisely, we should be clear enough that the dichotomy in the anthropological literature had plenty to do with the unresolved problem in the mighty discipline, namely economics. What we should consider, I pursue, is the lack in the framework of studying modern societies from the conventional economics point of view, which the anthropological theses became a reaction to. Consumption demands to be seen as a social process, as it was exemplified by Appadurai (1986), and that was never the case in the academic courses and programs of economics in Bangladesh.

Construction of Foreign and *Swadeshi*[2] Commodity

In a typically Southern precondition like the one Bangladesh has, the value of the commodities largely differs in regards to their origin. Among others, the most significant reason must be the general belief that emerged from an endless assertion that the newly formed nation-states were lacking in the production necessary for a modern way of life. It is then the common sense for

---

[1] This is to say that the significance Polyani's work (1958) created on the onset of widely accepted economics-tools into anthropological investigations and the general assertion it was able to generate of looking back into the uncritical appropriation of those categories.

[2] The reason I am using here the Bengali/Hindi word to mean local product it to deliberately associate it to: a) the movement of boycotting British commodities as a form of resisting British colonial rulers no matter what it could in turn carry out; b) the slogan of the government of Bangladesh for fairly a long period to promote the small scale production that took place under state supervision. Roughly the word can be translated as indigenous or local, in some specific cases as national too.

capable buyers at a particular moment to look for foreign goods when and where they find it to be necessary. However, the whole process of making the necessary commodities available to the buyers ends up with a huge paradox when it comes to the items that had already been manufactured in the local sectors or by the local companies. Keeping in mind the fact that the consumers would hardly bother the complex process of manufacturing, importing or marketing a commodity, we can figure out the dilemma the state had to go through in promoting a certain local good simultaneously with a comparable foreign one. Creating two distinct sets of values appears to be the dilemma. It could best be understood with the phrase 'politics of value'. [3]

Understandably, the concept of value put here surpasses the obvious meaning of cost or even price, as they are illustrated in the discussions of economics. Value should be seen here as a discursive domain that is not created exclusively in what is conceived as utility, but merely in the ideas and concepts manifested in the "words.[4] What I intend to illustrate here is that the commodities in the newly emerged nation-state of Bangladesh have incisively been categorized into foreign and local (*swadeshi*) ones – both from the promotional point of view and in the submissive responses towards it. These categories, hence discursive practices, which in turn form a sharp binary opposition, had plenty to do with the idea of 'foreign' itself – as an imaginative space with tremendous comfort, as a discrete journey of the unidentified desires, and as a comprehensive provocation for securing advantages. Further, it is also my intention not to mix up this phase with what I would call the 'brand-band', a tendency developed in recent times. Instead, I would like to distinguish the early phase solely in its separating principles and the tensions coming out of a conflicting binary.

In regard to the specific process of the dichotomy, it seems to be helpful to characterize the principles of construction in the early years of independent Bangladesh – roughly the first two decades since independence in 1971. These are general observations, but could appear as significant threads to realize the current investigation:

First, there had been a sharp distinction between the hardware products used for building infrastructure and the consumer products purposed for everyday usage, especially by the well-off people. Consequently, the dividing constructional process of foreign and local goods entailed the latter kind of products.

Second, while foreign goods surely meant for 'pride' and 'status', they left the consumers with a dubious feeling of lack of 'patriotism'. Consuming local products had long been associated with the meaning of being a patriot.

---

[3] Appadurai, Arjun "Introduction: commodities and the politics of value," in Arjun Appadurai ed. *The Social Life of Things*, Cambridge: Cambridge University Press, 1986
[4] ibid, p. 2.

Regardless of how the state machinery operates in a certain context for importing and promoting foreign goods, it was required from the government's point of view to 'protect' the 'interest' of local goods and/or manufacturers. Almost without exception, the government would deploy rhetoric to promote local goods.[5]

Third, foreign goods are meant to be the costly ones, thus a testimony of the upper-level consumption. It secured the prestige for those who afforded it.

Fourth, a sense of contest was evident in securing the space. It was about one's loyalty to the homeland. Those who deliberately avoided using foreign goods in everyday life, or could not afford it, had a fairly good chance to contest the users of those items. This especially had been a case in a domestic environment when both parties had to meet in social gatherings.

Fifth, foreign goods were also meant to be a sign of mobility since the local market was not providing all the desired commodities at that time. On the other hand, the same sign could reveal a sense of pressure for tentative 'smuggling', a moral category rather than a legal category in the middle-class conscience.

These are some general observations from the early years in Bangladesh before the policies for massive importing took place. But, on necessarily a middle-class consumerist onset, these could provide us with a comprehensive understanding of how the foreign and *swadeshi* goods signified distinct meanings and how they came to construct contesting spaces, and thus intended making of a nation in the early era of consumerism in Bangladesh – till the mid-80s since independence.

It is interesting, at this point, to take a clear account of what were the possible areas of commodities that had a contested meaning. Already it is mentioned that the hardware products, necessary for industrial purposes and purchased outside the domestic sphere, were out of any concern. Truly, it is an area that the popular nationalists, along with the left, are always arguing for. To develop a national industry with 'own' materials is being campaigned for what they believe is the actual 'independence.' This should not, for instance, be treated as it is being said; rather needs a set of critical investigative tools to unpack the rhetoric of these utterances to place it historically. My purpose here, however, is not relevant to this issue. For some obvious reasons, I am not considering the

---

[5] Until recently the most popular slogan was: *Swadeshi ponyo, kine how dhonyo"* [consume local products, and be proud]. It is not to say that this kind of rhetoric had anything to do with the actual picture of consumption. However, this particular slogan was largely associated with the cottage industry-products and handcrafts. In the later years, interesting enough, the rhetoric was seized even by the local fashion and beauty manufacturers.

hardware products of the ones consumed for industrial or agronomical purposes. In brief, these are not the overt areas where the discursive practices keep a significant mark in terms of everyday consumerism. Concerning the gross middle-class lifestyles, then, the domestic sphere commodities are the only concern of contestation. Electrical and electronic goods, since they were not manufactured locally for long and until recently, should also be kept aside for approaching the early phase of discursive formation. Artistic and literary products that should include books, films and music must not be in the tally since they were not under any dividing principles and were taken for granted as the obvious intellectual feed for the middle-class cultured self.[6] So we can find the rest easily. There remain more or less four types of commodities then: clothes and costumes, cosmetics and toiletries, utensils and home-decoration pieces, and foods and beverages.

Listing in this manner has a necessary provocation of inviting criticism for being too crude. But I would like to argue that it is of utmost importance to identify the products separately for having a better understanding of the resemblance of the people associated with it. These are the tangible and concrete references for their psychological attributes, for their emotional attachments. To explore the spatial and temporal meaning of what is perceived as "fetishism" in Marxist literature (Marx 1976), I maintain that this classification is of significance. Further, my position is that the process of the making of *swadesh* in comparison with the foreign is subtly related to the forms of consumption of these goods. Here consumption should not be understood in a mere utilitarian way, instead about the concept of value discussed above.

While all these four areas had been a subject of intense contestation – both in the assertion of pride on the one hand and in the celebration of loyalty on the other – it appeared to be a serious positional crisis in the following years when foreign goods started coming from the developing nations too. Earlier it was only the first nations' products that were available as foreign goods. Among them, cosmetics and toiletries are the kind at stake since a number of transnational cosmetic brands are now being manufactured locally. A sense of tension among the consumers could be found more intensely in the case of electronic and electric productions. Collaborative manufacturing is quite a familiar way to secure more business interests both for multinational and local companies. This is the case in contemporary Bangladesh too. Eventually, the

---

[6] The only exception took place in the recent times when, not by the camps categorically known as fundamentalists, but by some of the literary groups among middle class launched campaign against Indian Bengali publisher Ananda Publishers Pvt. Ltd. Though discontinued within a short period after initiated, it could be an interesting event to analyze. But scope of this chapter does not allow this act.

tension was about how these products should be defined – as local or as foreign. I insist on this point firmly because I would like to give attention to the discontinuity of the brand-craze thesis. A prestigious brand that collaborated with the local labor market cannot always remain as 'prestigious' as it had been before. The fact is evident, for example, in recent times with brands like Sharp or Toshiba from Japan or even Whirlpool from the US – the ones that started manufacturing from the plants located in Bangladesh.

Durability Discourse

In my view, the discourse of durability is a significant area to approach contemporary consumerism in Bangladesh. Although prestige had always been a crucial concern for well-off consumers, the durability discourse marked the early phase for encountering foreign goods in Bangladesh. With a closer look, one can be sure that there are two distinct implications of this discourse. First, it has the potential to refer to the politico-historical process of the globe, with special relevance to the former socialist nations' products on a global scale and the triumph surrounding it, relatively in a suppressed manner, among the consumers of the majority world (Third World probably is more appropriate in this case). Second, it claims the merit of offering a lead towards the huge shift of attitudes to foreign goods in general, and luxury goods in particular. Though it was not until the Chinese products came onto the scene that durability discourse could really be firm in place, the very idea of durable foreign goods existed for a long. The origin of this discourse seems to be rooted in the colonial period and with the emergence of native manufacturers of consumer goods as a mode of the *swadeshi* movement. It should be seen, I propose, as a justification to, and assertion of, the commodity products from the colonialist nation in general. All four types of commodities that I mentioned earlier came out as industrial products during the colonial period and under the colonial finance administration. Among others, one of the main responses by the colonial subjects was to build a network of commodities of their own since defying the process of industrialization could not be seen as a viable option. However, this background has its own merit to be discussed and analyzed separately.

I know this observation could be contested severely. It is really difficult to explore the things I am engaging here considering the lack of research literature when it is concerned with consumerism in Bangladesh. The methodological crisis appears. But such attempts like this one, I believe, can initiate a possible breakthrough for approaching the issues. I mentioned Chinese products as to be a crucial reference to the discourse of durability. It is an irony to the extent that not very diverse kinds of products really came from China. Within the mid-70s, Chinese products spread all over Bangladesh. Unlike the prestigious commodities, these are meant to be accessible to relatively marginal middle-class people, especially in small towns. Among the four types of commodities, Chinese products are only supplied at best in the two – clothes and utensils. To take a fair account, the most familiar Chinese products in Bangladesh can best be known as stationery goods like pins, staplers, tapes, blades, pens, pencils, colors and so on. Porcelain products must be treated as another substantial example of a Chinese image that has its grounds long back in the colonial period. It is not incidental that the porcelain is translated in Bengali as *Cheena Mati* (clay from China). Considering the textile products, Chinese fabrics scored huge. The name of this foreign nation became identical to some of their products which continue to be marketed till the present day. Initially branded for their cotton fabrics called Chinese poplin, it extended in the latter years as polyester, linen and nylon. An in-depth field study shows that the most popular item that had been in hype during the late 70s and early 80s, and specifically among the salaried small-town dwellers, was poplin and 'tetron' – perhaps a word in local invention to distinguish a finer type of cloth. But the triumph that was cashed by the 'China' image, and literally in every corner of Bangladesh, was related to a completely different product outside the categories I mentioned earlier. It was a bicycle branded as 'Phoenix'. If I were to select a singular commodity from China to testify what I am contending as durability discourse, I would go for this. Substantiating my argument, I must place the fact that for nearly two decades, this product meant to be a desire across the class and, in some cases, more profoundly, in the marginal social people.[7]

While I was arguing that Chinese products have been largely associated with the marginal middle-class people or among small-town dwellers, I also meant to say that the discursive formation of commodities was not necessarily, and consistently, founded upon the prestige goods or the costly brands, but on the mass attitudes towards the products sometimes. Further, it is also my position that the formation of discourses has not always had a linear nature but could be approached in a process of several contestations as well as a series of conformations – for example, while some people might assert the importance of consuming local goods for what they believe is good for the national economy, the other could have a similarly strong position for the cheaper goods regardless of its origin. My central argument here is that the durability discourse employed to characterize foreign goods was different from the newer discursive field that came out in the latter years, but the whole discursive field

---

[7] Referring to the 'dowry' system in the marriage transaction in Bangladesh, Phoenix cycle had long been a cherished by the rural people. I would like to note that 'dowry' in marriages of well-off people is always a complex thing to investigate because of its subtle nature. But for the rural poor people it is apparent and straight. According to my understanding, Phoenix bicycle marked the anonymity to the transaction of dowry itself.

about foreign commodities should be seen as an integral process and the former – i.e., durability discourse – must be seen as a necessary ascendant to the latter – i.e., prestige or brand discourse. And not surprisingly, the latter should be seen as the captor of the former. Since the central project was to classify and judge the local and foreign goods, the project provided a substantial foundation in the future years of excessive consumption in the enhancement of similar classification. It must be noticed that, like the early phase of commodity goods in colonial India, the early years in the independent state of Bangladesh asked for utilitarian justifications for the commodities. Chinese products could best befit for symbolizing the core urge for 'quality' and 'convenience' in this regard.[8]

Shopping Malls and New Consumerism

If the durability-discourse marks the early years' association with foreign goods in Bangladesh, the contemporary trend should be perceived grossly as the discourse of taste. In illustrating the contemporary trend, however, the huge scale in middle-class consumption should be noticed as the bottom line. This is to say that the discourse of taste itself cannot validate the massive consumption among the middle class. Nor does it stand for a good explanation for the vast expansion of consumer commodities – both foreign and local – simultaneously in the expansion of tangible shopping centers. Further, the discourse is not sufficient enough to give a clue for examining the growing desire to consume goods. In this line, the desire to consume is monumental among consumers in different parts of the globe. More or less, phrases like 'global middle-class' or 'cosmopolitan consumer' could comprehensibly be communicated and perceived in the present time (for example, Featherstone 1990). Accordingly, the complex nature of the political economy of the contemporary production process, especially that linked with different locales beyond a single national boundary, demands specific investigative tools and analyses. Also, we need to study the multifaceted and subtle consumers' behavior, or 'culture', if it would put across the proper meaning, of this age. What I mean here, with specific reference to the taste discourse, is that there was a shift in association with and representation of foreign commodities. And the shift appears to be significant.

During the 90s, specifically in the mid, the Dhaka cartography had changed drastically. The newly made shopping malls started marking the major characteristics of Dhaka. Being the capital city and arguably a metropolitan, Dhaka has always been likely to pass through new processes of urbanization. The recent phase, with plenty of multi-stored shopping malls all over the places

---

[8] With a critical look, it can be said that the English word 'quality' became an everyday term even among the commoners. It has something to do with the act of qualifying commodities in commoners' lexical.

in Dhaka is being exhibited as a prosperous feature in the city life and a sign of development. In most cases, each shopping complex contains as many kinds of products as it can compile together. The individual shops are supposed to be in the defined category of commodities – for instance, cosmetics, fashion-wear, jewelry, footwear, electronics, electrical, crafts, and what are promoted as gift items, groceries, fast-foods, ice-creams, pastries and bakeries and so on. Most strikingly, one can find the categorization is the basis of the credibility of a given shopping complex, no matter whether different shops in the complex are financed by separate investors or the entire complex by a single investor. Further, it is necessary to note that the obvious uniqueness of a complex or mall is its capacity to manifest some of the transnational brands famous for a particular genre of products – Peter England or Van Heusen for male garments, Pierre Cardin or Carbon for jewelry and Personi or L'Oréal for cosmetics. What is important here is the prior knowledge of the probable consumers of the products on a certain point and level. The fact reveals a serious advertising industry across the national border, which appears to be a concern of the current chapter. But at the same time it is not possible to explore the details of the industry in terms of its organization and process. In a general manner, we can evaluate the importance of this factor, along with others, into what I would like to characterize as the mode of consumption.

A comprehensive framework for approaching consumption was suggested in Prof. Ritzer and Stillman's work (2001). Famous for his McDonaldization theory, Ritzer furthered the ideas of means of consumption placed by Marx. Putting parallel to Marxist understanding of the means of production, he suggests that "means of consumption can be found in the concept of the means of production. The means of production occupy an intermediate position between workers and products; we need a sense of the means of consumption that occupy a similarly intermediate position between consumers and commodities. Thus, the means of consumption can be defined as those things, especially settings, that allow consumers access to commodities; they allow consumers to consume."[9] It is now needless to say that Ritzer's work is of utmost thought-provoking, which I am going to discuss later. The reason I am not engaging with Ritzer's historic

---

[9] Ritzer, George and Stillman, Todd, "The Modern Las Vegas Casino-Hotel: The Paradigmatic New Means of Consumption," *M@n@gement* [Special Issue: Deconstructing Las Vegas], Vol. 4, No. 3, Toronto: University of Toronto, 2001, pp. 83-99 http://www.dmsp.dauphine.fr/Management/. Although the work was done by Ritzer and Stillman, but I am mentioning only Ritzer's name. This has to do with the fact that Ritzer is already familiar for his theorization of consumption and has actually supplied for the framework for the work mentioned here too. However, the conceptualization they adopted was formulated in another work by him – Ritzer, George, *Enchanting a Disenchanted World: Revolutionizing the Means of Consumption,* Thousand Oaks, CA: Pine Forge Press, 1999.

work (1996), instead with the less renowned one, is that my purpose lies elsewhere. The conceptual framework generated in the mentioned work, very comprehensive and articulate, stands potential for future research work as a sound foundation. From here on, Ritzer, along with Stillman, went to engage with the Weberian concepts and tools. What is most interesting in their conceptualization is the accreditation of the settings that surround consumption. Seemingly, the idea of settings gives a sense of physicality. But a closer look into it opens the possibility to explore certain social preconditions in which the consumption takes place both as a physical action and a psychological reaction.

It is merely fascinating to observe that the hype of shopping malls started exactly in the period that was propagated as the democratic era in the Bangladeshi political process.[10] Though it is not an easy task to examine any such direct association of these two phenomena, the necessary provocation of liberal democratic norms has long been asserted with the capability of buying goods. Indeed, the very idea of empowerment is solely reduced to the discrete category of 'choice', even when it comes to the question of the lower-class population. In this line, the association between the democratic era of Bangladesh and the emergence of enormous shopping malls has something beyond a metaphoric meaning. Celebration of the 'choice' is being more and more perceived and insisted too as a political category for measuring people's freedom on a democratic standard. However, the prejudices that form the basis of an uncritical model of probing – mostly in the development literature – are serious and encompassing ones. The discourse of taste has little connection with choice. But we could unpack the meaning of choice, both as a set of crucial judgments of the products and as a series of acts to concretize that, in the vivacity of taste, of course, on the onset of the middle-class people, whom we can define as a cosmopolitan class for its certain attributes found beyond a national boundary. I would like to correlate the role of political processes, at least with concise hints, at the end of this essay.

'Brand-Band', Individuation and Identity Formation

I am a little afraid of being too ambitious in proposing the current argument, as it has already been mentioned that the main pressure came from the background of a lack of literature that engages with the Bangladeshi situation. However, to proceed to the final phase, here I would like to address the probable relationship between the prestigious brands and the people – the consumers of those brand items. Further, I would like to reflect on the possible framework for approaching this relationship in the context of identity formation.

---

[10] This is to mention the period since 1991 when electoral parliamentary system was established after a long-term military dictatorship of Lt. Gen. Ershad collapsed.

By using the term 'band', I refer exactly to the similar attributes that were classified and illustrated by the early colonial anthropologists (Fortes and Evans-Pritchard 1940, for instance) to define the political system of what they discovered as the primitive people. The term is used to refer to the simplest form of affiliation to a common identity and set of interests of the members of a group. Similarly, I would like to propose that contemporary brand fetishism provides us with a commonality of having a particular desire and pride altogether in the consumer of a particular good. This should be examined in the daily discourses of how the consumers portray their desire, loyalty and sense of pride in using a particular commodity. It can be easily pointed out when the discussion is about a commodity like television, and one can find a brand like Sony in the Bangladeshi case. But this may not be so clear to point out in some other events like when it comes to the question of jewelry or perfume. The desire is sharp and, at the same time, subtle which is conceded in a significant mass from the mentioned social class. It is the very desire (to consume and for taste), to my understanding, that forms the basis of the band.

Although foreign goods are solely mentioned here as the referent of prestige, a comprehensive understanding of present-day middle-class attitudes towards the invented 'traditional' and 'indigenous' commodities is necessary. This should not be perceived as a discontinuity to the hypothesis enhanced; rather should be seen as an extension to it. Since most of the prestigious 'traditional' pieces are connected in the global market, it has been securing the idea of foreign too. There are plenty of local agents, including the mighty Brac, known for its pro-poor microcredit programs and what is being defined as development activities, who for years have been promoting the Bangladeshi 'traditional' commodities among the local well-off people and the global market. One must be critical in perceiving the implications of these products. These mean to establish avenues for the cosmopolitan desire and the ever-renewed discovery of *swadesh*. These were enacted to carry the pride, of course, of a certain group of people to the imagined space of foreign, finally securing their desire on a global scale. In this process, the very sense of emancipation feeds the core formation of a band. I would like to maintain that the entire bunch of *swadeshi* commodities, mostly crafts and fabrics these days, plays as a single brand item and finally adds to the desired catalog for consumption. At this level, the meaning of foreign surpasses the physical origin of a product, but intermingles with the probable consumers across the globe, preferably referring to the White consumers of these.

Common assumption – the individual is contradictory to the group – resists the possibility of exploring the complex relationship between individuals and the brand bands. Living under the regime of comfort and within a realm of desire secures the individual spaces along with a potential bond of consumerhood among the consumers. A sense of anxiety is obvious within the process. Incapability to purchase a certain kind of good, or exhibiting a particular set of tastes, keeps the individual and the household in a sense of distress. On the other hand, it is the desire to own the good that keeps endless possibilities for them to be in the terrain. It means to be in a complex situation allowing oneself to be in a continuous imagination of possessing specific brands. The desire to consume appears as a testimony for the individual entity. Further, I contend identifying with the definite desire, for a defined brand, allows one to form an identity, a discrete mode of engineering the modern self, even in the huge chaos of commodity. This is where the promotional – hence advertisements in an old term – claim importance. The idea of customization, as it is propagated from the promoters' point of view, could best be read as a set of acts that enable to stimulate the desire.

Appropriating 'Foreign' in the Defined Nation: The Mode of Consumption

The idea of nation, in the process of consumption, seems to be located in the narrow corridor provided by the consumer goods. More precisely, it appears to be fabricated through the convenience of the availability of foreign goods. For a fairly long period, my field experience shows that this is how the nation should be perceived when it comes to the question of gross consumption in Bangladesh, especially in accordance with that of the middle class. But the apparent location does not necessarily explain the domination of the idea of a nation, or crudely of nationalism. So, we need to have a more critical and efficient framework while we are to engage with the idea of the nation. And specifically, the question of the mentioned desire comes seriously. What is, then, the location of the desire to manifest the nation?

Unlike Prof. Ritzer, I do not rely solely on the conceptualization of means of consumption. Referring to the situation of a Southern nation like Bangladesh, it is of utmost necessary to further the project by encountering a viable way out. But in the end, it is Prof. Ritzer's framework that provides us with the tools to reorganize the framework. Putting specific attention to the settings that actualize consumption, he exceeded Marx's categorical understanding of the means of consumption. It is the concern for settings that made Ritzer's theorization a distinct one. Comparing it to Marx's model of the mode of production, Ritzer came to what could best be fit with relations of consumption. I am well aware of the fact that the classification that arises here might miserably seem a schematic one. But it has some serious implications if we consider it in a certain location. The processes and components that Ritzer pointed out had founded a base for associating the desires of the consumers. Contemporary consumerism must be identified with a desperate desire to consume. But this has nothing to do with a direct and functional relationship with the act of consuming. Hence the relationship should be seen as a complex one. On the one hand, the ever-forming desire is a direct result of promotions and commercials, an aspect of what Ritzer explained as settings of consumption. On the other hand, the desire provides a space with the possibility for exploring and asserting newer goods. Within this complex relationship, the desire along with the means of production – the hardcore commodities as Marx perceived and the settings as Ritzer furthered – forms the consumption force. Schematically, again, I would like to posit desire as the most powerful component of the consumption force.

Far from being a physical location, the nation appears to be a set of principles and rules where the desire could be originated, nurtured, enhanced and furthered. Instrumentality that is identical to a nation-state sets a firm basis where the subjects of modern commodities can emerge and, in turn, can invalidate the principles and rules themselves to the extent where norms and morals rule over the formers. In this line, if we are to concentrate on the Bangladeshi situation, even genres like principles and rules became irrelevant to specific cases. For crude examples, it is the norms that drive the Chinese products out of the imagined foreign or the desired taste; it is the morals that can violently demand prestigious goods as 'rights' which can even clash with a governmental decree of preventing some foreign brands, even if it happens in our wildest imagination. Protection of rights in the form of celebrating 'choice' has its merit in the current discussion. Here, in a Southern condition like Bangladesh, the political process has a significant role. The overt meaning of liberal democracy may invite plenty of quotations from textbooks or from Western leaders' speeches who are willing to do good, no matter how, for the rest of the world, but the very meaning of it should be examined in specific ways in different locations. When it comes to the question of consumerism in Bangladesh, the meaning of liberal democracy is being reduced to the 'choice' of the middle-class consumers, too. In this line, relations of consumption entail a set of political institutions, namely democracy, as it is being perceived. Nation appears to manifest the prosperity, the availability of certain kinds of goods – that is to say, comfort and pride. The construction process of the nation entails a series of categories, motifs and gestures – all to substantiate a space, a system too, where the desires can be posited.

Chapter 4

The Politics of Secularism

This chapter tends to underline the current political terrain of Bangladesh where religion appears to be a significant instrument, this way or that, to govern the political vocabularies and manifest the reality. This statement above does not appeal a great deal considering the overemphasis in the global media on what they supposedly found as 'religious fundamentalism'. Unlike the conventional and dominant version, I like to argue something drastically different. My main concern here is the usage of religion as a decisive category to undermine the significant political processes, no matter if they are deliberated or conspiratory. I would like to remain clear that mine is not a task of detection, but rather to comprehend the social process for understanding beyond the apparent and the obvious. This is how, I suppose, the popularizing project in the political domain could be understood. In this attempt, I intend to discern actions of and around a significant event.

An Unprecedented Undercurrent Play

On June 21, 2002, the then President of Bangladesh, Prof. A. Q. M. Badruddoza Chowdhury, resigned from his office with a prior letter to Prime Minister Begum Khaleda Zia in response, inevitable though, to the insistence the leaders of the ruling parliamentary party BNP had shown in the previous two days' house-meetings. He was charged, at least officially, for discrediting the late Ziaur Rahman, an army general who was the founder of BNP, as the President did not pay a visit to the grave on the death anniversary of Zia. Prof. Chowdhury, on the other hand, was underlining the fact that the expected act was not a protocol for the presidential post, but instead a transgression of what he perceived as 'neutrality'. Understandably, Prof. Chowdhury's stance was available in those few pages only where the editors preferred to accommodate it. Just to avoid confusion, Prof. Chowdhury had also been a top-level BNP leader, and the utmost deputy of Zia's venture at the time of founding a political party. This is where the credibility of Prof. Chowdhury had been secured, within the party and among the public discussions, for more than two decades, until the dramatic removal at the end. Removal of a President like this, yet by the party itself, which had nominated him earlier, is unprecedented till today.

Flabbergasted by the event, the mass[1] readers of the newspapers followed the news of the event for the next few days, and then got laid back – no matter why, very soon fixed themselves back to their public and private involvements. Finally, they decided not to engage with, or explore further, the exemplary event. They remained somewhat happy with the lazy news follow-ups and allowed their daily discussions to have a little portion of reviewing the issue. No serious explanation was demanded. No petition was signed. Nobody, to my knowledge, filed a case against this unprecedented move by the government. Nor even any such urge was found to question the newspapers that were critically investigating the event. National dailies, on the other hand, literally duplicated the claim made by the BNP, which was already broadcast by the party officials, with recently achieved public relations skills. The only major exception was that of accommodating one or two 'exclusive' interviews of the ex-president. To be sure of its significance, he best tried to glorify the virtue of 'neutrality', by publicizing that he did what he felt to be 'right' and he was happy that he could show the testimony of 'democratic values,' and he resigned instead of 'compromising' with the narrow party-interests. Also, he expressed faith in the 'mass' that they would be able to judge his actions. The ex-president said nothing practically outside what already had been set as a framework by the government (BNP). The newspapers did nothing further, and the whole venture was about reassuring the claim of the BNP. No investigative pieces were published that could illustrate convincingly the motives of the actors. All these made the ruling party vulnerable for being 'incapable' of upholding democratic values, and thus remaining neutral. However, I believe that the consequences must be read beyond their apparent meanings. This fact might need a careful reading that within the next few days Tareq Zia, son of late Ziaur Rahman, was selected as the joint secretary-general of BNP. This was a remarkable event that was publicized with great effort and managed to generate substantial jubilation among the party youngsters – all over the country.

I understand the *actors* of the event were simply successful by being able to keep the people very much within the pre-designed boundary of information. What I think is very important to explore here is how public amnesia is enormously significant for an understanding of the present political and social processes in Bangladesh. I intend to explore here this public (read middle-

---

[1] I am sure that this concept is confusing for the readers, especially in a Southern condition. 'Mass' does not refer to a uniform category of people. Nor does it stand with de facto usage as it been has claimed to be. Here the best I could do is to restrict its meaning within the boundary of the readers – educated and middle class (as it is defined in the first chapter). But there was no chance to avoid the concept since it has an overt meaning of agency.

class) reaction in regard to the mounting claim of 'religious fundamentalism' in Bangladesh. My intention is not, by any means, to undermine the current situation or the threats that are being perceived in different corners of Bangladesh. Nor do I mean to cancel out any possibility of a 'take over' that could tentatively be named as a 'fundamentalist' uprising. That is, in my consideration, absolutely a different question and needs to get a distinct set of investigative tools.[2] What I would like to analyze is the basis of the gross assumption of Islamic fundamentalism and its inner technologies of comforting a middle-class self – of reducing the sense of social insecurity into a discrete category that has been 'alien', and as a matter of fact 'other' to the very construction of 'cultured self.' In this line, it is necessary to comprehend the global, and diasporic too, nature of the 'self' that is the architect of the current form of discovering terror, reducing its meaning to a manageable category of 'other' – an armed opponent for the sake of one's own 'struggle', literally a virtue for the contemporary cosmopolitan middle-class. To make a brief connection with the event I mentioned at the opening, let us think of some speculative questions, vital though. Why is this that the people felt comfortable with only a little knowledge about the President's removal? What prevented them from asking for a comprehensible explanation from the press? Does not it give an idea about their firm understanding of an undercurrent power play? Why, then, did they keep silent? And why do they, on the contrary, expect more and more stories about the 'fundamentalists'? Why is this that they are not interested in exploring some power pools, whereas they are very much focused on exploring the others? And, how does the press, along with some other agencies, play a crucial role in shaping public interest in general and providing readers with a guideline in particular? Do the secular movements dare to challenge militancy?

---

[2] The common tendency of dismissing the possibility of an Islamist uprising in Bangladesh is associated with the heterogeneous cultural background of the country. This has fairly been a claim from the secular middle class in reference to the history and in comparison with the Middle-Eastern nations, and to some extent, contemporary India too. This comparison, until very recently, reveals a sense of pride for having 'more' secularist values in the society. I found, however, this claim a vague justification for progressive norms and poor understanding of modern nation-state. Keeping in mind the Indian case, one must be sure of the huge potentials of apparently a weaker political group to take over the state power. Considering their bluntly adopted liberalization policies – economic and beyond – I am doubtful, however, in perceiving BJP's rise as a case of 'fundamentalist' uprising.

An Awkward Collaboration between the Left and the Liberal

Like many other nations, academia and the press are crucial in shaping public perceptions. There is nothing new in this proposition.[3] What I intend to further here is that the role of academia in the West is covert to some extent, whereas in a nation like Bangladesh, often academic institutions are overt places of politicking. One of the many manifestations is the selection of vice-chancellors of the state-financed universities from hardcore interest groups, mostly out of any convincing academic concerns. This tendency marked the feature of present days Bangladesh but needs to be put aside in this discussion.

Although the secularists could be able to indicate significant oppositional sects they encounter in academia, on the other hand, it must be recognized that a thorough basis for their political desire has been established through academic activities – within the academic institutions and beyond its boundaries, namely in the developmental processes. In my understanding, the utmost result appeared in the channel between the left and the liberals regarding conceiving self and others. These two camps, even during the 70s, had plenty of points to disagree with. Now they finally found themselves very close in some specific issues. I do realize the overall political situation around the globe that enhances the possibility. But this is not a question of justifying one's vulnerability, but rather dealing with its consequences. However, this proximity resulted in a huge unprotected space for the religious 'other' to occupy as opposition. I would like to illustrate this process into two distinct phases: 1) The students' activities and/or movements that came to be a decisive generator of political vocabularies, thus actions, once again during the 80s; 2) The emergence of civil society and developmental discourses, specifically during the 90s.

It is generally perceived in Bangladesh that students' activities during the 80s were a massive one. This has been compared to the events of the late 60s. Encouraged by the overall middle-class disappointment with the military rule and General Ershad,[4] students' movement marked a significant clash with the governments in different forums. Eventually, Ershad had to introduce a militant students' wing for in-campus to chase off the active student groups. However, the

---

[3] Reasonably, this is a gross illustration of the proposal made by Chomsky (along with Herman).
Chomsky, Noam and Herman, Edward S. *Manufacturing Consent: The Political Economy of Mass Media*. London and New York: Verso, 2002.
[4] Lt. Gen. H. M. Ershad was a military dictator in Bangladesh from 1981 to 1990 after the killing of Maj. Gen. Ziaur Rahman, another military junta turned popular icon of Bangladeshi politics. Ershad, later, was one of the key founders of some political parties and finally decided to be the chief of Jatiya Party [National Party]. Currently he is leading one of the streams of JP and holding a member-of-parliament position.

obvious feature of students' movements is much discussed and can be illustrated further. Most striking was the emergence of some supposedly left students' group[5] besides the former ones[6], which very soon appeared to be a strong force – both in its strong voice in the political vocabularies and militant roles on the university campuses. Although their main target was Ershad and the military regime, they faced a series of clashes with the *Islami Chhatra Shibir*, the student wing of Jamaat-e-Islami[7], which had been gaining more and more power at the time. Certainly, these clashes have their distinct meanings in the history of Bangladeshi students' politics. More than that, I would like to point my finger at the vast hatred generated against *Islami Chhatra Shibir* [ICS] in particular, but interestingly against anything 'Islamic' in general during this time. How far this reduction is significant may be revealed in the next section. The brutality of ICS is a serious issue for sure, which must not be undermined. But this was not something confined to ICS in the campus history of Bangladesh till the present day. ICS had constantly been charged with being 'fundamentalist', a discrete category that emerged already, with a value-judged connotation and without any concrete political reference. What I mean here is a very simple one. There is much commonality among the students' political groups – left and other liberal right-wingers – concerning the perception of ICS and reducing Islamists in Bangladesh into its entity. Apart from challenging the Ershad regime, the students' movement during the 80s set a public attitude, I argue, for approaching Islamic groups, and it went far beyond the boundaries of campuses.

Compared to the former, the second phase is much more complicated and has multiple implications. It started, apparently, with the initiative[8] taken for bringing the war criminals under punishment just after the fall of Ershad and the BNP's win in the parliamentary election. The most quoted event was that of the *Gono Adalat* (peoples' court) on March 1992, where the prosecutors, with

---

[5] for example, *Biplobi Chhatro Moitree* [revolutionary students' union].
[6] for example, Bangladesh Students' Union or JSD Students' League.
[7] Jamaat-e-Islami is a political party in Bangladesh securing 4th position in the parliament. Currently they are in coalition with the government having two cabinet posts. This party mostly has been referred to with 'fundamentalism' in Bangladesh. Actually, for more than a decade they were synonymous to 'fundamentalism' [*moulobad*]. Formed during the Pakistan period, this party officially supported the military brutality by Pakistan against Bangladesh, and informally organized killings of thousands of Bangladeshis during and after the liberation war. Also they supported the US intervention into the war of independence of baking up Pakistan.
[8] A public forum was formed for this purpose in 1992 – *Ghatak Dalal Nirmul Committee* [Committee for Eliminating Killers and Collaborators]. This was able to create massive sensation among the middle class people, and especially the metropolitan ones, and has been an active group in the later years.

the public consent, as was propagated, announced mock punishment to the notorious war criminals – the majority of whom were the members of Jamaat-e-Islami along with a few from other political parties. However, the activities of this camp were not limited only to the *Gono Adalat* event. Campaigning all over the country took place. Leaflets were published, wall-writings were straight and frequent, and publications were made – all in support of the claim of bringing the war criminals under legal action. Soon, the sensation went across the national border, and the activists came to a confronting situation with the then government. This, however, was the first ever exposed agitation regarding the war criminals of 1971. Despite its mobility and power the movement was never able to upset the targets and is believed to be a failure, even by its interlocutors. Partly because of the strong backing the BNP government then showed to the targets, then because of the electoral and other party interests that Awami League, as a major stakeholder of the movement, executed in the following years. These factors are well discussed too and I like to push it further and to remain skeptical by joining the chorus of assessing the movement as a failure.

If we seriously consider the power of discourses, then the significance of this movement during the early 90s lies elsewhere and must be understood in its utmost capacity of generating a new set of vocabularies, of drawing demarcation line between what was seemingly a proper social stance or what was not, of pointing out the 'fundamentalism' as the sole opposition, eventually of being confused about a suitable stance about Islamism, and finally of constructing a space comfortable for different agents, inevitably from the middle-class. It is not to say that these were all deliberate agendas from the organizers' point of view, but surely were the consequences of their activities. Thus, the decisive outcome went far away from singling out the war criminals no matter what punishment they might go under. The outcome was about an overarching discourse of 'fundamentalism', which was followed by the claim of dissociating Islam in every visible social matter – overtly in the public discussion, and covertly in the middle-class desire. This, I believe, laid a substantial foundation for Bangladeshi politics in the latter days, especially the politics of secularism. Yet the deceiving failure – of not being able to bring the criminals under punishment – was caused by a different factor, I contend. This was the very hype of 'civil society' that was created among the middle class very soon. Referring to the first chapter, by 'civil society' here, I do mean the organizations and agencies consisting of a middle-class population in Bangladesh and are self-claiming about their leadership in certain issues. Further, I would like to continue that it was meant to be a mishmash for the liberals and the left. Engineered by transnational agencies and local NGOs,⁹ formation of the 'civil society' was a trajectory in the political processes of Bangladesh. In search of a reasonable foundation, I uphold that the rise of the *Ghatak Dalal Nirmul Committee* had to do something with the concept and activities of 'civil society' in the 90s. It was just a phase when many social and political forums were looking for a space to posit their voices. With its own merits, the question of war criminals in Bangladesh, an unresolved issue for years, was found to be a viable issue. So it was a call for bringing them under prosecution, a gross call made by the leading secular middle-class agencies that meant to create a nationalist sentiment across social boundaries.[10]

I do not mean to say that 'civil society' was a homogenous forum; instead, I am well aware of the challenges and criticism from some of the left groups towards the emerging concept and activities of 'civil society'. What I mean to say is twofold: first, the newly conceived activities founded a more liberal basis of the middle-class mobility where different groups, including the left, relapsed; secondly, ideas about and discourses of the 'development' vigorously invaded the political desire of the middle-class. This is to say, referring to my point, the collaboration of leftists and liberals. 'Development' is meant to be a mandatory process, an indispensable term in everyday usage regardless of the different political positions among the groups within the middle class. Liberals, mostly from the NGOs, wrote their agendas of development, and the lefts their own. Hardly had they come out from different epistemological planes. Integral to the discourses of development was its imagined opponent – the 'backwards' and the forces that could lead the nation to 'backwardness.' It was, then, only a processual journey for the 'religious' to take place.

Jamaat-e-Islami: An Enemy Improperly-Marked

The portrayal of Jamaat-e-Islami [JI], right from the beginning, caused a serious crisis in assessing the Islamic theological movements and their political implications. Secular forces in Bangladesh have always pinpointed what they perceived as the religious nature of this party and condemned it for mixing up religion with politics. This is paradoxical. One must be aware of finding the root of this blending – religion with politics – long back in the colonial policies, of

---

[9] Both the categories – 'civil society' and 'NGO' – are difficult to use in an international readership. By definition they hardly bear any difference among them and across nations. But firstly, NGOs' entity is definite and should be read distinctively regardless of the huge overlapping space these two share. And secondly, the meaning of each category, functionally, differs a lot even in the neighboring nations.

[10] My position was further illustrated in my polemical piece in Bengali. *Unmochon*, No. 3, Dhaka.

which the secular force is itself a product, too. I do not anticipate elaborating on this here just as a precaution of irrelevance, but I surely would like to refer to, in brief, the deliberate introduction of Shari'a laws and Hindu inheritance laws by the British colonizers, especially at a time when the entire region was first experiencing a systematic, mandatory too, transformation towards a centralized state.[11] Historically, this was never a serious point of agitation from the secularists, no matter what that would mean.

Referring back to the issue of portraying JI, secularist forces kept on charging this party of combining religion with politics. This accusation has laid the foundation of discussions about Islamism-in-public-sphere and fundamentalism, specifically, whatever that means at a certain historical point. With the fact of its emergence as the sole political group with Islamic claims after the decline of the Muslim League, we must keep in mind the importance of this political party in independent Bangladesh. My point is not to undermine their role, but instead the opposite. I just mean to underline the fact that JI was hardly charged for maintaining an alliance with the Pakistani military, materially arranging the killings, for denying the idea of independence unless Bangladesh achieved it. Once again, I do not assert that the secularist camps were homogenous and that no one was involved in any kind of activities I am referring to here. To be more precise, I am pointing here that the dominant mode of portraying JI in independent Bangladesh and by the secularist camps was about associating them with Islamism. This kind of act, I further contend, in no way helped either to chase their horrible role, before and after the independence of Bangladesh, nor did it help to develop a proper framework by and large to examine the Islamists in Bangladesh. On the contrary, this could only generate an undefined hatred against anything related to religion[12] in the public sphere.

Therefore, instead of seeing this phase as a challenge to, or a criticism of, JI I am much interested in seeing it as an avenue of portraying the religious 'other', as well as the secular 'self' – of course, in a dichotomous way. The ultimate

---

[11] See Asad's works on this:
Asad, Talal. *Some Aspects of Change in the Structure of the Muslim Family in the Punjub Under British Rule*. Oxford: University of Oxford [unpublished B.Lit. thesis], 1961;
Asad, Talal. "Conscripts of Civilization," in C. W. Gailey, Ed, *Civilization in Crisis*, vol.1 of Dialectical Anthropology: Essays in Honour of Stanley Diamond, pp. 333-51. Gainesville: University of Florida Press, 1992.
[12] Actually Islam, in case of Bangladesh, or even anywhere. It could be merely interesting to note that most of the Bangladeshi secular middle class people associate themselves with various religious motifs – for example statuette of Buddha, Ganesh, Krishna or Mary. Hardly one finds it religious. But when it comes with a signature of Islam, i.e. a photo of Kab'a Sharif, they just cannot stand it. I believe much depends on the discursive formation, and not always only to the 'religion' itself.

success was to reduce JI, and later on, other political groups related to Islam, into a category already defined across the nations. Eventually, this meant to be a parameter either to accept a political group, or to reject it. But JI's role historically can never be caught within the boundary of the definite meaning of fundamentalism, or in the binary of secularist-fundamentalist. Understandably, the very recent global events and an arrogant US call for 'war against terror' just increased the importance of the category of fundamentalism, and this is yet to be proved as harmful to the JI interests. We must note the hardcore pro-US campaign this party has been launching for years. I have very little doubt that the effective portrayal by the secularists, initiated after Bangladesh's independence and accelerated since the 80s, made JI just comfortable. They have been allowed to remain as one of the many Islamist groups around the globe and within the country – more importantly, some of these are actively anti-imperialist.[13] Oversimplification of the framework often minimizes any possibility of reading the Islamist trends in different corners of Bangladesh. Moreover, it damaged the popular spirit of religious scholarship that has been central to Bangladeshi society for centuries. Not only did it assist missions of the forces like JI, but it also provided just a little space for religious scholarship to make its ground. Finally, this tendency forced the religious 'other' only to enact themselves in a defined way of reacting. It must be understood that no Islamist group is capable of retaining a coalition with JI in contemporary Bangladesh. This is not because they necessarily feel closer to JI, but because this is the only option left for them within the allocated political space.[14] The secularist middle-class intelligentsia must be marked as an active cartographer of contemporary political spaces. The discursive formation that they had fabricated for years – within the academia and around the public forums – has its principles of incorporating certain factors, while preventing others.

---

[13] One key tendency to solve the relation between imperialism and religious political groups is to depict the latter as a product of the former, and finally to dismiss the both. As if, a dismissal can reduce commentators' responsibility to perceive the contemporary social processes. This is especially a framework popular among the left intellectuals. Whatever evidences this claim entails, it seems to be, academically, ridiculous. Often they refer to the Taliban case and it reveals more absurdities with the fact of exceptional atrocities that they faced from the US authority. Polemically I pose, well; Muslim League in undivided India was a product of Indian Congress. So, who is going to dismiss its political significance?

[14] A case might be interesting. Despite no evidence, even JI faced a serious crisis of inner-party uprising while the US invaded Afghanistan in 2001. Led by the party youth, this uprising demanded for a clear stance from the officials against US invasion. JI had to work hard to manage this uprising with some on-street demonstrations followed by a series of diplomatic make-ups. This is part of the many untold stories and really hard to verify since the press was never able to cover the events.

The 'OIC Trick'

Nominating Salahuddin Quader Chowdhury [SQC] for the OIC [Organization of Islamic Countries] secretary-general post was a significant move. He is well documented as a war criminal and somehow managed to legally escape any challenge regardless of the regimes since 1971, the year of Bangladeshi independence. Despite the apparent glee all over the opposition camps, including the Awami League, left political groups, and even some anonymous officials of the ruling BNP for his defeat, I think the event was not appropriately analyzed. He was said to have close ties with the defined fundamentalist groups, which appears to be a formulaic allegation and far from his capacity. His nomination should be seen, as I like to argue, as directly connected to, and successive of, the removal of Prof. Chowdhury. Surely, one can suggest that the public discussion among the secularist forums also spot on this. That is, they perceived Prof. Chowdhury as a sensitive person to secular values and SQC as the opposite. This could have a ground, of course, but I would like to point to four possibilities, of course, for asserting what I do anticipate: 1. SQC is not just a politician only. According to the press source also, as a trader he is believed to have connections across the national border and beyond the typical legal boundary. 2. His nomination should not be seen as a gross BNP act as such. One must be able to explore or assess interest groups within and beyond BNP. 3. SQC and his anonymous allies desperately needed an official role *de facto* for some projects still unknown, especially in the turmoil of the Middle-Eastern situation. 4. The same oligarchy also needed Prof. Chowdhury removed, as he had built a strong network among political activists. The anonymous oligarchy needed a President without political party background, and who would remain solely within the economic issues.

This is something that needs to be examined beyond the convenient method of discovering terror in the 'fundamentalist'. While a number of events are happening in a row, one cannot afford the amateurish reluctance to those. It is unfeasible, in my understanding, to come up with an issue like 'terror' and 'terrorization' and to seal off simultaneously the avenues of the power-plays. Never was it a sole question of religious, political groups, or for instance, 'fundamentalists' in a more acceptable category when it comes to terrorization and militancy – especially in a Southern nation like Bangladesh, and more specifically during the contemporary time. My intention is not to muddle up the things. I just am underlining the ease of identifying the boogeymen as 'terror'. I am worried about allowing too much loose space for the agents still unmarked.

Emergence of Corporate Groups

Emerging corporate groups are central to the political processes we are referring to and must be understood seriously. It might seem disconnected from the query we commenced with, namely secularism. But since the question is to explore the rise of militancy in contemporary Bangladesh, I consider ties and alliances that are being ignored and remain veiled in need to be taken critically. This is not to say that these ties came out of the blue, nor is to say that militancy is a new phenomenon. However, the recent intensification of the violent attacks[15] is a point of reference, and this is where the 'religious militant groups' are being identified as the actors.

In recent years, one of the most violent episodes is the series of evictions of the slums. I mention it to recall the enormous capacity of the newly organized finance groups and their newly ventured business projects like multi-stored housing and shopping malls. Further, I would like to figure out their strong bondage with the press, not only to the fact that the press, during the last two decades, was exclusively taken over by the corporate groups, but also to the fact that the evictions had a prior middle-class consciousness about the necessity of evicting. Slums were portrayed as the place of 'corruption', 'illegal drugs and addiction-materials trade', 'sex trade' and so on. The absurdity of this claim was never challenged. Never was it a sensible case of exploring the actors behind the scene even if the claim had some basis at all. Never did anyone ask for any good explanation of how the poor people could be genuine traders and, at the same time, allow themselves to be evicted on one fine morning. The press kept on their role of demonizing the slums, whereas the middle-class people were relieved by the eviction. Most paradoxical was the fact that, with very few exceptions, most of the multi-stored buildings were constructed by the nearby source of labor from these slums. I do not intend to illustrate these events further but only up to the point that the commercial investor groups are gaining more and more power.

Taking the housing projects just as a reference, the investigation could be extended to banking, insurance, health services, entertainment and so on. While I am focused on noticing the connection of corporate groups in the current political situation, I would not be interested in perceiving the relationship among the emerging groups as 'class solidarity'.

---

[15] The recent phase is considered with the series of attacks since the bombing in the *Udichi* conference five years back. *Udichi* is a nation-wide social-cultural organization backed by the Communist Party. This attack was followed by the attacks in CPB meeting, Chhayanat Bangla new year's program, a series of cinema hall attacks, then attack on Awami League meeting on 21 August 2004 where Ivy Rahaman was killed, finally the recent attack on AL meeting in Sylhet where ex-finance minister S M S Kibria was killed. But these are all the 'big' events which the press covered. There has been a plenty of other attacks and killings – isolated incidents and killings by the state-agencies.

It is commonsensical that interest groups often cross the class boundaries. Relationships among the corporate groups can hardly be uncovered. First of all, they are not just local or national. Secondly, they are operating extra-legal. Thirdly, the use of terror is essential for their activities. Fourthly, they are to clash with each other to gain control of the emerging space.[16] I do not think that the middle-class people are not in a position to comprehend these facts, but are not willing to. That is where the importance of the current investigation lies. With very little available information, examples might be extracted, like harassment of the *Jamuna* group or television channel *Ekushey*. I do not mean to undermine whatever legal discontinuity they might have as it is being propagated; what I mean to say is that the turmoil appears only when a competitive faction is designed to execute it.

Religion as a Secular Weapon

I deliberately posed a question earlier: Do the secular movements dare to challenge militancy? Just to refer to the contentment they show in serial killings by the state agencies. This is a difficult attempt in the contemporary globe – posing a question that defies the norms. The obvious provocation in the specified dichotomy of 'fundamentalism-secularism' is to limit our search only to the binary. But, reviewing the current events in Bangladesh, this appears to be too unconvincing. Firmly, I would like to be doubtful about the politics of secularism in Bangladesh, for it has been successful in silencing a lot of social issues as illustrated in this chapter – of demonizing what it believed consistently as its opponents, for portraying a self that is full of liberal attributes – politics of secularism must be, academically, taken critically. This is what my intention in this chapter is. I am sure that there are substantial implications of this scheme in other regions of, typically defined, South Asia. This is not, however, sensible to attempt a comparison right now.[17]

One aspect of taking the right track in the current search is to investigate the middle-class prejudices against religious matters, Islamic matters in particular, that were attained historically. This is not an easy task, though. Generally, the task is to question the very hypersensitivity to seeing religion in the public sphere. More specifically, the inquiry is about how Islamism means 'evil'.

---

[16] I think, categorically, relationships among the corporate groups can best be defined as 'oligarchy'. I used the term in doing so in my recent Bengali piece. *Yogayog*, No. 7, Dhaka, 2005.
[17] For example the analyses Ashis Nandy (1985) put with a careful posture of what he calls as 'anti-secularist'. On the other hand, not many scholars from the same region would like to tally with him. Rather, most of the critical stances that are coming out from Indian scholars are engaged mainly to find out the problems of realizing secularism and renovate it.

Further, it never cancels out the immediate task of unpacking the power networks that constantly penetrate the sense of insecurity – of the state-backed agencies, the overt and formal ones, the covert and undefined ones, their transnational counterparts, complex interest groups that include interests like overseas trades, arms deals, smuggling, sex industry, media industry, property development and so on. There are religious groups, for sure. No point in overlooking the possibility of these groups' gaining power. There is Jamaat-e-Islami. They proved to be a mighty event-maker in the last four decades. But one should not be ignorant about the mightiest agencies in the very recent Bangladesh. The politics of secularism in Bangladesh is acting just in the way the power-actors had foreseen it. Within the continuous production of decisive categories and knowledge, middle-class reluctance is comprehensible. But what I am concerned about is the academics' and intelligentsia's luxury of reducing their understanding into the discrete and vague hypothesis of 'fundamentalism' that appears almost every day in the press and public discussions.

This is what I tried to figure out as the use of religion as a decisive instrument to undermine crucial political events, mostly undercurrent though. I am much aware of the deductive nature of my claim. At the same time, the emphasis on a tentative 'fundamentalism' reduces every possibility of comprehending the Bangladeshi power network. The cases analyzed in this chapter – first the removal of the president and its press coverage, then the OIC management strategies by the underworld power network and its lack of presence in the media and the public discussions, and finally, the overall construction of Islamism – are all related to each other and show how the broader middle-class people are reluctant to cruise into the deep-rooted facts in Bangladesh and how the construction process of popular phenomena is successful in certain ways. The overall middle-class inertia towards engaging with the political process on a deeper level, compared to their hyperactivity in pointing at the 'fundamentalism', marks the popular phenomenon of contemporary Bangladesh.

Chapter 5

'Lawful' Heroes and 'Terrorist' Villains

There must be a 'National' Film?

This chapter seeks to deal with the discursive formation upon which the images of the heroes in the recent popular films[1] of Bangladesh are constructed. It is confusing these days to use a single term for this particular trend in Bangladeshi films. Alternatively, the phrase 'mainstream films' refers to as connotes the same trend. In both occasions, they are referred to as the products of the state-owned film industry, in the case of Bangladesh. And those films are believed to be consumed by the working-class people, hence the non-educated ones. One major problem of using the latter, even to some degree, the former, is its foundational presumption of the dichotomy of 'good' and 'bad' films. That is: what is 'popular' or 'mainstream' is surely lacking *taste* in regard to a high-art standard set by the educated middle-class audience. So these terms deployed in an oppositional meaning towards what is believed to be the 'art' or 'parallel' films, is meant to be an intellectual product. In a Gramscian understanding, things are more complicated. Gramsci perceived 'popular' as referring to somewhat a sense of counter-hegemony contesting the dominant system (Gramsci 1973). This perception does not seem capable of handling the complexities of modern popularizing projects. Further, there could be some good reasons for adopting the term 'public culture' in this regard. Pinney found 'popular' a problematic term and opted for what Appadurai and Breckenridge suggested back (Pinney 2001). Since Bangladeshi film productions have defined and differentiated audiences, I opted for the term 'popular'.

It is common knowledge that these images are ever-changing, depending on the dominant concepts and ideas of masculinity at a particular moment. In this line, core principles of constructing a hero have always been justified, in a subtle manner, with the parameters that came out to be the testimony of a 'good guy'. With only a few exceptions, this has been the trend of Bangladeshi popular films. Here I do not intend to unfold the very meaning of 'goodness' since that is a different assignment altogether. I intend to critically look into the emergence of discourses like 'lawfulness' and 'terrorism' and their influence in

---

[1] For a comprehensible account, popular films in Bangladeshi contexts are referred solely to the films produced under the Film Development Corporation [FDC], a state organ to monitor film production. That is to say, the films having a larger marketing strategy are to be referred to as popular films according to the middle class and media vocabularies.

shaping the representation of a Hero. In other words, the intrinsic strategies to cope with the changes in portraying a hero in popular Bangladeshi films are at the heart of my concern.

Popular films or mainstream films, in regards to Bangladesh, can be referred to solely as the products of the film industry under the Film Development Corporation [FDC] – an autonomous but state-nominated body for supervising film production. FDC was established under the Pakistani state in 1957. After the independence of Bangladesh, it was entitled to the Bangladesh government. Ideally, the main responsibility of FDC is to provide the atmosphere and technological facilities that are necessary for film production, a process run by the independent financiers are experts who are in the business. But the term 'FDC' seems to connote a more generic sense in the middle-class public discussions in Bangladesh. It demeans the genre produced through this chain on a 'taste' ground. While this has been a consistent attitude in the last two decades, the first few years after independence are marked to be promising for the middle-class intelligentsia. Filmmakers like Zahir Raihan, Alamgir Kabir and Khan Ata in the initial phase were pioneering the effort. There took place some huge changes for what the critics certainly can claim some points.

On one hand, the number of annual production of films increased from an approximate average of 30 per year during the mid-70s to 70 in the late 80s (Hayat 1987). Now the films produced in a year are averaging over 100. On the other hand, both in terms of storyline and visual styles, recent films are loud, flat, and what is termed as 'vulgar', and eventually, are facing a total refusal from the educated middle-class audience. This trend has been set roughly from the mid-80s. So, the viewers of these films are, by and large, the urban working-class people along with the categorically defined illiterate people in small towns and rural areas. Considering the power and immensity of the Mumbai film industry, the Bangladeshi situation is drastically different. I do not mean to evaluate on the qualitative ground, since that must not be the purpose of this attempt. But since the Indian films are referred to so often, and are from the same region, I just wanted to note that the viewers of Hindi films are versatile, and they are consumed across the social classes. Although it is not in the scope of this study, I would like to hint that the Indian situation may have a connection with their dominant, historically middle-class culture, which is currently being endorsed by an enormous diasporic community, too. Films appeared as a feasible entertainment for the strata we are talking about. While this has never been the case in Bangladesh, there were clues at the time of this research (during 2004-2006) that the financial groups are approaching the middle-class entertainment zone. These are, however, not going to be explored further in the current attempt, nor even the genre named 'art' or 'parallel' films – in opposition to commercial or mainstream films, as mentioned earlier.[2]

The films are flat and monotonous in many ways – from representation styles to storylines, from casting to advertising and also in the film titles. Titles, however, are fascinating to catalog in terms of their nuances. For the typical love stories and family-drama, the titles range from – 'Tumi Kar' [Whom do you belong to], 'Premer Joyar' [Flood of love], 'Ghor-shongshar' [Home and conjugality], 'Shukher shongshar' [Sweet home], 'Baba Keno Chakor' [Why is father a servant], 'Shami Keno Ashami' [Why is the husband in accusation] etc. On the other hand, the action cinemas, necessarily with love affairs in-built, entail a kind of more vicious expression – 'Shonghorsho' [Fight], 'Palabi Kothai' [Where would you escape], 'Ajker Hangama' [Turmoil of these days], 'Danga' [Clash], 'Khun' [Murder] and so on. All the titles from these recent films have already been marketed in the last 7/8 years. Mechanical reproduction and dullness are just obvious there with the overt and cliché sexualizing effort. In this sense, the middle-class discomfort with these films can be comprehensible. But that is not the crucial point of the whole film issue. What I am more concerned of, and eventually would like to contend, is that the discomfort ends up ruling the entertainment world of the 'other' class – both in terms of their denial towards the entire genre without any attempts to provide some alternatives and in regards to the middle-class project of legitimizing the sentiments and agony.

At this point, I encountered two methodological problems, which I guess are bothering a number of academics, especially from the South. This is about the anticipated boundary of the national film. In every aspect, contemporary cultural products are being taken into the discussion mainly on the parameter of a national boundary. This surely has certain obvious logic and conveniences. Not only is it embedded into the sense of national culture and identity from a native point of view, but also in the specific mode of readership across the national border that seems to have a defined and expert point of view, of course, a global one. I am unsure, accordingly, if the categorization helps us at all with a proper understanding of any kind of cultural products, hence films, of a specific location. Considering the contemporary global network, it is only

---

[2] I had some observations made years back (in 2000) in a daily newspaper in Bengali regarding the mounting middle class criticism of the mainstream films and FDC. While I had no such intention to the kind of products the film industry had produced, my interest was to unmask the middle-class insecurity and their will to rule the entertainment arena in general, the visual world in particular. Also I hinted about the possibility of new kinds of visual products specifically for the educated and 'cultured' people (Chowdhury 2001 b). The recent trend insists the merit of my speculation. A number of finance groups are into the film business and are organizing different setups including different studios outside FDC, media labs, new projection houses like cineplexes and so on.

possible to discuss it relationally[3]. In brief, certainly, there are films that could unconditionally be defined as 'Bangladeshi' concerning its production process and authorizing body, but it is hardly feasible to anticipate any investigation of the 'Bangladeshi' culture as such. The tendency to assess an 'indigenous' culture through its films is a continued practice in the world of academia. The second methodological problem concerns the lack of research on Bangladeshi mainstream films. Studying films never appeared to be a serious venture in broader social sciences or communication studies in Bangladesh. Only a handful of works have been conducted recently, mostly under the communication and the journalism discipline and none of those seemed to be relevant in the current search. This fact can be justified by my experience of lecturing or teaching, not incidentally, in three prominent journalism programs in different institutions in Bangladesh. However, these works have mainly analyzed the representation of women in popular films.

Before its incorporation under the Bangladeshi state, the Film Development Corporation had a background in making films in Urdu and Bengali languages. The concept of sentimentality, however, was central to the early films in Bangladesh. But the utmost feature must be underlined with the dichotomy of masculinity and femininity which was firmly placed as the foundational principle of making the storylines. Although Hollywood movies were a factor, they did not influence the early Bangladeshi films by a great deal. Instead, it looked for a style from the films released by the then-Calcutta film industry and then-Bombay film industry. It must be understood that both in the Calcutta and Bombay films, the dominant genres shared many commonalities in regard to the plots, sentiments, familial ideologies, and above all, the dichotomous positioning of males and females – i.e., love affairs among the younger people from well-off backgrounds, tensions in the joint family, despair of migrating to the city life, contesting the 'evil' forces in society, loyalty of Indian women and so on. This is rather a general outset that heroes were supposed to be calm and family-oriented in particular contexts. Independent Bangladesh provided a relatively extensive space for making local language-based films while the filmic genre remained fairly similar. These films, plotted in different social locations, were able to generate a certain level of viewership across the classes with a large number of middle-class audiences in their course.

---

[3] It is merely apparent now that writing for an international audience on rather a local form of cultural product inevitably bears a pressure of introducing so many things that could prevent the flow of any observation. A level of readership is helpful for approaching a topic like the one I encounter. For instance, if it is the case with Indian film, the international academic audiences have quite a modest preparation to get engaged with the issues. Being an anthropologist, it is really hard to assume the commonalities that are at hand in different locations. At the same time, I am convinced that there are the commonalities to begin with a possible reading.

***Vinashaya Cha Dushkrita*[4] Emergence of the Action Heroes**

It should be marked that the armed struggle for the independence of Bangladesh created a specific atmosphere for the emergence of action heroes. Unlike films in other sub-continental nations, Bangladeshi films, as I like to propose, did not need to follow the radical political processes for their inception of action heroes. If the early films could grossly be marked for the overt familial ideologies, the metamorphosis of the filmic genres can easily be traced into the line of 'social consciousnesses'. It appears to be a sharp irony that the very revealing of 'violence' can best be studied in the outlet of this revealing of 'social'. I would like to refrain from judging a particular genre over others. And that is not an easy task either. To proceed into the current discussion one must notice the contested arguments both these archetypes entail against each other. The viewers of the former category – those improvising 'familial values' – have arguments for nurturing the emotions and sentiments, which, as they advocate, are necessary for upholding morals and, above all, the family. And the viewers of the latter – those improvising the 'social responsibilities' – have arguments for caring for justice and social equity.

Undoubtedly, the observations made above can be criticized on the basis that these may seem irrelevant when considering the lack of subscription amongst the overall educated middle-class of, what I categorically call, mainstream films. But the obvious capacity of the films – both as an entertainment sector for the lower strata people and as a vehicle of middle-class norms and values – places them as major cultural products that must be analyzed. However, the reasons that make me feel that there is a need for a serious analysis of this matter lie elsewhere. Whereas the shift in the filmic genres – e.g., in the narratives, thus the visualizations, caused a remarkable rearrangement in the portrayal of the heroes, the images of the heroines, comparatively, remained unaltered. This, I contend, is of utmost necessity in comprehending the gender dichotomy in both genres – familial cinemas and social cinema. Keeping female characters within a set and stable style of representation eased up the mechanism of creating much more vibrant heroes in contrast. Since the current chapter attempts to explore masculine images, I would remain disengaged with the making of feminine images in this particular trend. Here, we are taking into account the latter trends of heroes in Bangladeshi films where they are supposed to bear concerns about the 'social'[5] – the action heroes.

---

[4] *Srimadvaghabat Gita*, Here I have a little observation. Besides other influences, the Indian epical sensation have a stimulating role in dichotomizing the 'good' and 'evil' in the early films. At least it could also be read in this line.

[5] Often the heroes of the early times are mocked at by the consumers of the latter styles for their specifically less 'masculine' attributes, for having the 'lover-boy' images, for being too soft.

Making action heroes is a linear process. The hero is the fighter. At the root of an existing story and the narrative, he who fights stands out as a hero. Embedded into a series of attributes, fighting appears to be the marker of a hero, even if it is a visible fight for independence. The concept of fighting has an immediate meaning of physical acts which refer to the action cinema. But it surpasses the meaning to an abstract level of conceptualizing the struggle. This is to say that the filmic representation of a hero's struggle in a lifetime, along with his complex psychological and sexual affairs, signifies a specific virtue. At this point, the portrayal of a hero may transcend the defined boundary of an action cinema and consequently can accommodate other genres, such as representing a struggling hero. An attempt to outline a number of principles that are fundamental to the making of a hero would be useful.

a) Firstly, a hero is the combination of all the expected masculine attributes in a certain moment. Attributes such as 'courage', 'bravery', 'precise analysis', 'composure', 'control', 'self-expression' or 'rage', 'antipathy', and 'vengeance' are all there to reinforce the glory of being a male. This is not to say that an anti-image never appears, but this does not necessarily ensure any continuity for anti-hegemonic representation. On the contrary, anti-images often become the recurring symbols of manliness or an absence of a merely desired role, a prelude to the obvious metamorphosis and not a reminder of feminist consciousness.[6]

b) Secondly, a hero must have a series of obstacles in his life. The obstacles are manifold and multi-dimensional. He cannot be identified outside that domain; his distinctiveness is subjected to these impediments. One formula is to portray the hero as economically vulnerable. Poverty, in this case, appears to be an easy testimony to the barriers he will eventually challenge. If this is not the case within a narrative, then the theme is supplemented by other unavoidable factors. More often, the hero falls into unfavorable situations through sudden incidents.

c) Thirdly, a hero must be willing to accept the challenges. A man who is scared of, or hesitant, to these difficulties is not accredited to claim the

---

[6] Amit Rai (2005) at Florida State University brought forward a relevant question during the presentation of my paper on this issue. He referred to the recent trend of portraying 'less-masculine' heroes in Bollywood or Mumbai films and asked if Bangladesh had something comparable. Mainstream films in Bangladesh are yet to accommodate the trend. I think the recent standardization that is taking place in Indian cinema is largely related to its diasporic audiences – both as the consumer, but more importantly as the architect of literary consciousness within and beyond India.

heroic profile. It is one of the characteristics of the hero that he asserts himself to the challenges. Not only because his refusal to do so is a fatal blow to his manliness, but also because it limits his anticipated activities to the entitlements of an action cinema.

d) Fourthly, the whole process of facing the challenges opens up some significant avenues where the hero is supposed to build a social network across a certain social class or group. Referring to some early-fashioned narratives, a crucial presence might be of some priest, unspecific though, to inspire the morals of the hero. As these characters are declining these days, heroines often have taken the role of boosting male morale. But across-the-class networking is a feature that usually goes far beyond this personal meaning of stimulation. It must be underlined as a source of vital power that the heroes have been cherishing.

e) Fifthly, the hero's struggle has a particular social meaning. Hazardous situations that mark a hero's profile result from the active presence of a defined entity of the opponent. It might be an individual or a group of people – the villains. Unlike the heroes, these people do not have the public consent. That is a central mode of representation in Bangladeshi popular films.

These principles are fundamentals of, but not confined to, the action cinema. Whether or not the film entails an action hero mainly depends on the presence of the villain. This is almost obligatory without any exception. The hero and the villain have a formulaic structural relationship in the popular films of Bangladesh. How the space has been perceived and allocated in turn for specifying the hero and the villain, respectively, is a conditional question. Revealing this is necessary for examining the very recent tendency we are referring to.

A Case: Storyline of *Jhor*

Jhor [Storm] can be a good example as one of the many similar films. This entails the elements I am talking about – a hero who is for social justice, an 'honest' and soft-spoken person (a school teacher); a greedy and cruel villain; of course, a sequence of love-affair; and above all, the hero as a policeman. The school teacher is so 'honest' that he pays the fees for the students who are financially unable to pay. The hero once received similar help from this teacher during his secondary examination long back. Now the hero is in an anonymous 'town', serving as an 'inspector'. One must be clear that, in Bangladeshi mainstream films, 'towns' or 'villages' are hardly locatable and are usually referred to these generic and vague words. Also, the police-heroes are fixed on being 'inspectors'. Coming back to the storyline, the hero decides to join the police-station of the same village where he was a student. And he does so. He finds the corrupted police officials around who serve as the local 'gang-lord'. Then he visits his teacher with a wristwatch as a gift, as the teacher, years back, gave him his wristwatch to sell out for the tuition fees.

The teacher, after these many years, initially does not recognize him. Then, it turns out to be an emotional meeting. In the next few days, the hero falls in love with the daughter of his teacher. In this situation, films in Bangladesh must contain a series of songs and dances to visualize a love-affair. So, this is also the case here. Anyway, the teacher, as he is very honest, is requested by the 'dwellers' to contest the election and fight against the 'bad people.' But the villain wants someone else to get the nomination (from some anonymous party) and contest, because this is how he can maintain his doings. The villain and his followers threaten the teacher. But the teacher remains bold and gets nominated by some anonymous political party. Here, in this particular film, there are some twists. Some national leader comes to solve the problem and he is also an 'honest' politician. So he finds the teacher as the right candidate and finalizes his decision, and leaves the place for 'town'. Involving an imaginary national political party is not very common in the films, but these components are also coming out gradually. Later, the villain finds the 'inspector' to be a troublemaker and uses his 'influences' and 'connections' to transfer this police officer [the hero]. He has to leave. Then, we find the hero reading a newspaper to know that the teacher died. Somehow, he realizes that it was a murder, and voluntarily, he, with oral permission from the 'boss', decides to go there, head the police station, investigate the case and punish the criminals. Eventually, he beats up all the gangsters by himself, although the casualty on his part is a serious one – his lover-turned-into-wife gets injured, and the child inside her dies.

Good and Evil: The Wealthy Villain and Confrontation

Contrary to the varied portrayals of the heroes, the representation of a villain's character has been plain and simple in the popular films of Bangladesh, for decades. His first and foremost characteristic necessarily appears in his continuous efforts to create obstacles for the hero. An action from his end is usually formulated quite easily since the importance of the villain is much more comprehensive and comprehensible within the social relationships in comparison to the presence of other characters. What should be underlined here is that his capacity is not restricted only to creating obstacles for the hero; his fatalistic role goes so much against the hero that he harms the mass-people as well. For example, in these films, the villain, inevitably, is sexually aggressive – to the women generally but to the heroine in particular, and customarily is inclined to rape her. This tenet is structurally linked with the hero's capacity to attract the heroine differently. I do not, however, intend to detail it since this has not been a concern of the current exploration.

The villain appears to be anti-people through various events and role-play. The most vital one is possibly his hankering for wealth. He and his fellows (a group of leading villains only in some rare cases) accumulate wealth in many different ways. It is important to note that these many ways indicate either the exploitation of the working class, the violation of legal codes or both at the same time. In mainstream Bangladeshi films, it is hardly possible to think of a villain who is not very rich. Other villains with no money, the fellow supporters of the villain, are only complementary characters to the narrative. This is not to say that possessing wealth is the sole feature of him. He must be ruthless and greedy. In recent times, another feature is consistently being pushed and accredited as a depravity of his characteristics. For instance, he is an antagonist to the indigenous[7] culture. Though the villain entails a number of typical negative qualities, I am not going to single out every one of them. Among all his attributes, his being wealthy requires particular attention since this is meant to be a referring point to the people's interest. How wealth is represented in popular films is an important question for a firm understanding of a villain and, thus, of a hero. Further, it plays for a lead towards the domain of the hero's sovereignty that comes eventually as the course of the mass consent. It is the consent that allows a hero, an action hero specifically, to act in his gallant activities. To put it more critically, this consent has allowed the hero to contest the very relationship of wealth for a long period in Bangladeshi films.

The dichotomous nature of the framework with a wealthy villain and deprived hero indicates a formula in these films. Here, the binary appears to be a serious testimony of the hero's virtue, as well as the villain's evil. While the formula has long been nurtured conveniently in some cases, there are plenty of examples where it shifted. The hero does not necessarily have to be without wealth, as it is mandatory for the villain to be wealthy. Anyone from the hero's side is allowed to be a wealthy person. It might be his father, the heroine's father, and he or the heroine. There is a significant difference between the wealth that is permissible, and that is not. It must be noted that 'good people' could easily be accepted as rich persons either because they are believed not to be exploiting the working-class, or because they are not the antagonists of an anticipated indigenous culture, or because they are securing any presumed interest of the country. In this respect, it is relevant to refer to the gross idea of justice in the way it is revealed in these cinemas. Dichotomies of good and evil, or hero and villain,

---

[7] Understandably there are certain formulas for filmic representation of the supposedly 'indigenous'. It is popularly believed among the middle class people that mainstream films are hyped and worthless. It is interesting to note that the discourses of 'indigenous', and some times 'national', are very much same to that of the literate society, namely the middle class. While the indigenous has a sharp gendered space in the mainstream films, this is also common in middle class self-representation.

are all founded upon, and authorized by, the notion of justice. This is not to say that 'good'-wealthy people do not have social ties with the groups of people who are poor. Certainly, they do. But in these instances, poverty is a social relationship seemingly based on mutual consent. In other words, social endorsement is working here for the wealth – a consent of legitimizing the social relationship of property.[8] On the other hand, the villain remains vulnerable till the end since he does not owe it to the public. He, without having the endorsement by the common people, is to face a contest from them. The hero could be the best representative of their abhorrence. This is definitely the huge space that has long been allocated to the heroes in the action cinemas of Bangladesh.

At this point, I would like to make my position clear: Firstly, I do not mean to refer to all these observations in a historical manner or to push them in a seamless boundary; rather, the opposite is my intention. My attempt is to distinguish a few elements of Bangladeshi mainstream films in a specific period just to posit the recent changes that tend to invalidate the earlier style of representation. Secondly, in regard to the wealth-accumulation on the villain's part, it is not my scheme to propose any qualitative difference between the wealth amassed with social authorization and the wealth accumulated without it. Although there had never been hatred for, or protest against, the ways of accumulating wealth in these films in general, rather than being taken for granted and remaining unmarked by and large, there are certain discourses on wealth and 'proper' ways to grab it, which depict fairly a comprehensive sense of disapproval. I mean not only to say that this is where the villain, stereotypically, comes under sanction but also to the extent that this is one of the determining factors, if not the only, that allows the hero's probable activities and legitimizes those. Representation of wealth appears to be the foreground of contesting social relations in a resolution.

Thus, for some time, the villains have been depicted as the anti-people element mainly in an economic logic – exploiting the poor people, robbing or smuggling material things, etc. On the other hand, the competitive attitudes towards wealth have been exhibited initially through the hero's continuous status as economically vulnerable. Some of the narratives were typical, and of a specific kind, e.g., he might have been shown as not being able to bear his parents' medical expenses, or for instance, repair his houses etc. Or, it could be that the hero was having a horrible time getting a simple job. What is significant here is

---

[8] This is another example of how the mainstream films in Bangladesh are a crucial area of cultural products. Consent, here, appears to be critical to set a hegemonic notion of property. In my view, Bangladeshi films, despite of the simplistic denial of the middle-class people have been showing, are to be taken seriously for their extreme capacity of reconciliation.

that the villain, despite his huge resources collected through diverse means and a strong network apparently, was always crushed and destroyed by the hero. Villains may be of different origins – beginning from the feudal landlords or industrialists to the international traders – but nothing is adequate to protect them from the ultimate destiny. These villains are anti-people, thus 'evil', and seem to be instrumental in making the hero's life a living hell. Whereas the hero is a 'good' one and he is favored by the mass consensus, executing his monumental actions to revive the people's interest. His personal affairs, of course, heterosexual and highly significant, are juxtaposed within the framework. Acceptability of his mobility, I contend, had long been assured on the inner principle of contesting the wealth. Here, the meaning of the people has a subtle influence on the overt and crude exhibition of wealth.

Is *Desh* a Location of mass-People or an Entity of Legislature?

With the gallant heroes, the concept of *desh*[9] became integral to the narratives of the films. This outlines the shift from the earlier sentimental films towards what is being propagated as 'social action' films – that is, the films having stories propagating a kind of social justice or equity. The concept of *desh* provided the action heroes with the space they needed for the newly attained masculinity. In other words, *desh* became the imaginary, though authentic, space and set of relations for which the hero could execute his activities. To that extent, his action could well be defined as 'duties' or 'responsibilities' in a certain context. Doing something for the sake of *desh*, thus, not only represents his bravery but also a heroic virtue. This is not to say that this can be identified as an overt tendency, nor is it possible to crudely categorize the films with this trend. But this could be seen, I would like to maintain, as a schematic implication of a number of films in a considerable period till the present. Expecting the hero to do the Herculean jobs, the audience needs a good lead to his relationship with the *desh*. Nevertheless, they are a significant stakeholder in the relationship. The hero is supposed to be for their interests and for the sake of the *desh*, too. Accordingly, it seems necessary to actualize a sense of the physicality of the *desh*. Though exceptions are not absent, the meaning of *desh* does not consistently refer to the modern cartographic existence of Bangladesh.

It is, then, a process of exploring an entity of *desh* that is embedded into the styles of representations of these cinemas. Given the mass-consent we are referring to, the hero had long been allowed to pass through every corner of its imaginary space, to enact what he feels to be right, to occupy it literally, definitely with the mass endorsement of his probable actions. The space is

---

[9] *Desh* could grossly be translated as country or nation or motherland given on a certain context.

vibrant. It could seem easy at certain moments to point out the discourses on which the representation of the *desh*, and stylization of the heroes within its boundary has been materialized. But it probably is not as easy as it seems. If we seriously consider the production of the filmic genres, it was never an easy task for visual producers to discover the signifiers. To push their productions up to the comprehensibility and sustainability among the consumers was a further difficult matter, especially in the Bangladeshi context.

One manifestation of this concern might have been to frame it on the discourse of the 'mother nation'. The subcontinental attitude towards this discourse surely provided an assurance. Further, the war of independence in Bangladesh was a moral clue to this. Consequently, it was tested too in a number of films. It is relevant here to suggest a little about the Indian scenario. With specific reference to the films, since the blockbuster *Mother India* (1957), it is commonsensical to the audience that Indian films could refer comfortably to the notion of motherhood while engaging the nation. Though Indian nationalism has a particularly complex history and has passed through different phases, the discourses on nationalism never disprove the notion of motherhood. Even in contemporary days, it is being argued that the regeneration of Indian nationalism in post-colonial India is being juxtaposed to a series of iconographic representations of the nation, actually of the map at the end. Some writers insist, especially in regards to the visual media other than films, that the nation has been personified and thus iconized in certain forms of visual productions[10]. This is a thought-provoking idea, especially in case we attempt to analyze big hit TV serials like *Mahabharata* (1988-89, in 94 episodes in *Doordarshan*, the national TV channel of India) or the promotion for the national cricket team. In turn, it could be revealed that the nation as a mother has been deployed effectively in diverse visual products, especially in the popular print products consumed by larger lower-class people. Whatever the reasons are, specific forms of visual productions with particular icons were much flourished in the BJP regime, as it is argued in some cases, and it reassured the assumption of Hindu fundamentalism.[11]

Whatever merits this particular observation may have in its course of arguments, Bangladeshi films rarely were a reflection of this. Though there were indeed some popular films produced in Bangladesh just after its independence, picturizing some emotional outlets of the war of independence in 1971.

---

[10] A good example might be Brosius's work (Brosius 1997). She had indeed very interesting points, though exclusively about Indian situation. However she also went for the hypothesis of Hindu-fundamentalism. Just to note, I do not subscribe the idea that BJP could be understood within this defined category.
[11] Ibid.

Inevitably, the notion of 'mother' was an important factor in those films. To explore the probable background these films were based upon, we must critically examine the cultural production that took place during the war, and specifically in the radio broadcasting which was a significant catalyst for generating the emotional milieu for the war. It is also interesting to discover that Bangladeshi cultural manufacturers, as well as the products, fairly merged with the then-Calcutta cultural agents.[12] For example, the theatre activities found their cultural ties with those from Calcutta, or be it people from Bangladesh or Calcutta, the authentic Bengali culture was meant to be associated with *Shantiniketan*, a university and cultural universe founded by Rabindranath Tagore.

However, though there were some films that signified the nation as the 'mother', which were immersed in the emotionality of the war, these should not be considered a trendsetter for not having any consistency in the succeeding period. One reason might be that of the Hindu mythical backdrop that has not been relevant in the Bangladeshi context. But further examination of the factor might lead us to some understanding that transcends this singular assumption. Firstly, multiple interest groups had reasonably different interpretations, thus manifestations, of the war of independence, which is crudely represented in political vocabularies as 'for and against Bangladeshi independence.' The killing of Sheikh Mujibur Rahman, the nationalist political leader and the architect of the independence of Bangladesh in 1975, started severe political turmoil in the country that had shaken the linear production of cultural motifs. Referring to the war with the already framed viewership[13] was not possible anymore, if at all it was a priority of a particular film producer. Secondly, the sensibility to the modern cartographic arrangement was never in a position comparable even to other subcontinental nations like India or Pakistan. The Indian middle-class perceived their nation based on cartography long back, at least with the emergence of the National Congress in 1885, while the Pakistani middle-class did so during the emergence of the Muslim League in 1906. Thirdly, film production in Bangladesh suffered an early entry of middle-class norms and codes without prior training of the large viewers, which, in turn, was rejected.

---

[12] Examining this issue could be interesting in the emerging area of secularism-fundamentalism binary and their respective manifestations. Further, related though, it could also give a lead to the debate of pro-Indian and pro-Islamic/pro-Pakistani cultural productions in Bangladesh.

[13] I use the term 'viewership' to connote a systematic appropriation and appreciation of certain a filmic genre in a certain context. Therefore, it entails acts like following specific style of representation, decodifying the meanings of visual motifs and icons and so on; thus, implicating a manufacturer-consumer continuum. This is like the concept of readership as it has been used in contemporary critical literature.

Fourthly, certainly, there were crucial differences between the viewers' relations with the myths, legends, and folklore in Bangladesh and India. This relation should be treated as vital for connecting the people with the fundamental discourses on which visual production, hence film production, occurred.

Thus, my reading is that Bangladeshi popular films did not iconize the nation as a 'mother' at a level that can be referred to as a style of representation. Any concept comparable to *desh-matrika*[14] never appeared as a frequent notion or discourse. But this did not interrupt the process of representing the *desh* as a location of the mass people. Formation of the 'mass' in the kind of cinemas needed a definite historical thread. Looking back at its peoples' history of fighting for their rights or social equity, whatever that reveals on a certain trajectory, Bangladeshi films discovered a space for locating the ideas regarding the *desh*. The War of Independence played a very insignificant catalyst in it. Often this discovered space, and maintained too, transcended the border of Bangladesh, or rather became a vague clue for it. Moreover, people's struggle often surpassed any comprehensible link to specific historical references. Yet, my main purpose is not to look for any concrete reference but to point out the core framework of perceiving the *desh*. I maintain that this framework derived from a firm belief that 'the people' of the region had long been engaged in the struggle for social equity. It is the framework that provides the heroes a space to execute their extravagant activities.

A hero, on this backdrop, was allowed the space to freely move and do things up to the limit that tentatively transgresses a legal-moral boundary perceived in modern society. This is where the question of consent becomes so important. An Action hero was genuinely celebrating the people's endorsement of his actions without restraining him. He was not under any scrutiny of morality except for that of monogamy. Other than subscribing to the monogamous virtue, the only matter he needed to bother about was the interest of the 'masses'.

Until recently, heroic actions were secured within the meaning of *desh*, as I like to propose. A major shift occurred, in the contemporary film arena of Bangladesh, in the conception of the *desh*, and, subsequently, in the styles of representing the hero. In recent discourses, the *desh* is found as an entity of legislature and laws, and not merely as a location of the mass-people. On one hand, this shift is subtle and a tricky one. On the other hand, this necessitates a major shuffle in the narratives. Also, it entails a series of changes in the exhibition of the heroes, and thus of the villains too. For a very brief example, a villain, in this line, is 'evil' not because he plays against the people's interest, but because he plays against the laws. Accordingly, a hero is a hero because he is a devotee of the laws, and he is capable of bringing the villain under punishment.

---

[14] The literary expression of mother-nation in Bengali. Though a very bookish form, it should be used to refer to the representations we are discussing about.

However, I do not mean to say that the meaning of *desh* had the determining role of reorganizing the heroes. Instead, it is more likely that both readjustments are the outcome of ever-growing global sensibility towards the legal codes. Further, the recent renewed hype of 'terrorism' played a crucial role in this regard.

This is a situation of utmost difficulty in terms of the filmic representation of a hero. Restricting him from any probable extra-legal activities produced the tension of reduction in the space he was accredited with. It is a tension of minimizing his actions. Not that it reduced his activities always. But certainly, there are new strategies that are being taken to reassure his activities. It is interesting to see the various ways applied in this ironic situation from the manufacturers' point of view.

New Heroes: Liberal Nationalism and the Clutches of the Law

The discourse of 'lawfulness' should be considered as a major factor that is shaping the hero's charisma in the contemporary cinema of Bangladesh. This is, on the one hand, a response to the increasing civil consciousness of, and subscription to, the legal system – not always the established 'law and order situation' as it is being repeatedly uttered in the media, but to a vague outline of the middle-class desire. On the other hand, the filmic representation of the present heroes is itself an act of reassuring legal codes. It is meaningful to note that during the 90s, the law had become a matter of enormous celebration. Everyday public assertions of differentiating almost everything into 'legal or illegal' could be its crudest example, but a serious shift should be underlined.[15] This specific discursive formation inevitably affected the social space for the hero. (This tendency not only reduced the possibility for a kind of 'Robin Hood' image of the hero, it also threatened him with the absence of the mass consensus that previously had been the basis of his contest with the social relation of wealth and beyond.) Heroes are necessary either to get authorized by, or to be sanitized with, the legal discourses. In this line, 'terrorism' often has an overt meaning contrary to the earlier fluxes and 'heroism' remains on a very fragile boundary of 'lawful' and 'unlawful'.

Even the early films, indeed had to demonstrate certain conformities to the state law. Often, within the narratives of the action or the social cinema, some policeman of a government official and preferably a judge in the court would say, "do not take the law into your own hands." But never had it meant a distinct reduction in heroic activities. This was part of the preaching of so many things on 'national' issues. And there could be a number of heroes who vigorously deny the apparent simplicity of this claim and may deliver a full-length lecture

---

[15] It has something to do with the civil society movement that overtly took place since the early 90s. A much stated slogan that they carried out was 'rule of law.'

about how the state law was not adequate to abide by, about how it was discriminatory towards some social groups etc. Some pieces of evidence can be found, though not many, where the hero even accepted the challenge of chasing the legal authority at the cost of his life.[16]

Contrary to the situation, the 'police' are making more important appearances these days. To its limit, the hero himself is increasingly playing that very lawful role of the police. Or, in the case of a pair of heroes, one of them is usually a policeman. Incorporating the diverse characteristics of the hero's manliness and prowess, the 'policeman' image is gradually becoming a permissible social appearance. He is now allowed to exhibit his activities to the level of what an early hero was expected to do. At the same time, he is not under any pressure of transgressing the law. This must be seen as a readjustment to the discourses of lawfulness. Since anything extra-legal connotes 'terror' and the hero must not be a 'terrorist', finally, the styles of the representation seemingly reduce the possibility of being antagonists to the 'nation' or the 'national interest'. Laws are likely to appear as normative here rather than the substantial code of action. This is not to say that this is confined to Bangladesh only. Rather, the Mumbai films or the Hollywood films have the same stream of glorifying the legally authorized male images – the police or the military. And this must be analyzed in the global context of liberal norms. But, Bangladeshi films demand a specific treatment, too, because they do not have any particular referent to military activities that could 'glorify' a heroic profile in comparison to the US or India. The sole event was the War of Independence, which declined its viewership, as discussed before. Nationalism in Bangladesh does not necessarily provide visual motifs to the film industry that can be improvised or taken for granted as discursive formations for representing the heroes.

Yet again, the hero's position as a policeman is not the final factor. He may or may not be a policeman, but hardly this factor has any imperative in his attitudes towards the legal authority and the legislation. Hero is seen, at times, going through a process of sanitization or salvation despite his continuous valiant acts. It could include a mere voluntary surrender to the law not because the legal authority, i.e., the police force, chased him down under arrest, but because he felt a need to uphold the virtue of the law, because he meant to be a 'good citizen' of the nation. This particular process of sanitization of the hero, I argue, is a consequence of liberal nationalism. Ideas of the nation in necessarily a liberal society engage in discovering ever-renewable tenets. It should also be noticed that abiding by the law has become identical to patriotism where the social and material relationship of the mass people are no longer a significant

---

[16] Mumbai films have an exemplary tradition for that. The most popular one is probably *Akheri Rishta* acted by Amitabh Bachchan.

factor. The villain is not patriotic since he denies the boundary of the laws, because he earns money from extra-legal means of trading; the hero is patriotic since he is the opposite – the model may seem to be a simplistic one, but it has provided some underlining principle for representing the male characters. The utmost difficulties a hero is now having are that of the absence the social consent to do what is extra-legal. This consent, to some extent, is related to the revelation of the competitive relationship between the villain and the common people, of which property is a crucial element. A hero seems to have a hard time now concerning his manifestation of heroic acts and masculinity.

My purpose was not to generalize the contemporary representations of the heroes in Bangladeshi films, but to provide an account of certain aspects of the mainstream films there. On a relational aspect, images of heroes and ideas of masculinity are subject to continuing adjustments to the changes of the discursive formation, and at a global level for sure. What I urge here is the necessity for remaining critical enough to understand the very premises that lay the foundation of the replicas of local cartography.

Chapter 6

Environmentalism as a Global Consciousness

An Unusual Inception

The chapter faces an initial shock from some activities that developed very recently in contemporary Bangladesh in regard to the issue we are to engage in here. Just at the beginning of this research, in late 2004, the issue was incepted with an important assumption that campaigning against tobacco was not an immediate possibility in a Southern nation like Bangladesh. It appeared to be a drastically wrong idea only after a few days. On March 13, 2005, the government of Bangladesh passed a bill that bans smoking in public places and the advertisements of tobacco production like cigarettes in every media. This was certainly a response to FCTC[1], which hardly had been presumed before the act was taken. By and large, this move should be examined critically with its probable consequences, especially what it means to the very claim of 'tobacco control' and, eventually, the environmental consciousness. To its potential, this move should further be read on the backdrop of the political processes in Bangladesh and the influences of transnational agencies like WHO. It is a hard task, though, considering the specific nature of political discussions that hardly entail anything obscure.

Given their explicit nature of pro-environment advocacy in the current years, I had intended to explore the vocabularies and actions geared by BAT[2]. But the recent move by the state authority demands something special to its course. How a multinational business agency like BAT deployed specific vocabularies and actions with defined meanings and juxtaposed them in an environment-conscious framework was the main concern for me. It would merely be an interesting attempt to look into the means this agency adopts to come up with the recent actions – specifically the newly encountered inability to promote the products publicly. However, it is too early to measure the counter strategies

---

[1] World Health Organization Framework Convention on Tobacco Control.
[2] British American Tobacco. This multinational company started its venture in Bangladesh just after the independence, in 1971, as BTC [Bangladesh Tobacco Company]. The government had only a nominal share. In line of their global identity change, BTC later named as BAT on 1998.

from their end. What the recent move, after all, opens up is the necessity of examining the governmental actions.

This is not to say that the recent move overturns the importance of the discourses on environmentalism, instead the opposite. It is more relevant now than ever to explore why the Bangladeshi government, at a certain moment, felt it necessary to respond as what tentatively would be named as environmentally 'conscious', yet without any such 'civil' pressure of mobilization. To what extent this attempt is consistent with the overall environmental or health activities of the government, or for instance, of the state is another significant query to this examination. While these are the areas that became instant points of reference, I feel mostly inclined towards a separate inquiry, though associated with the previous ones. That is: how far the business agencies are potential stakeholders in this extraordinary decision. It should be clear that approaching the quest asks for extensive research on the matter of which this discussion could best be a modest introduction only, and not beyond that level at all. Further, it should be clear that despite its utmost significance, this particular attempt does not include the review of the presumable influence of, and the power generated by, the organizations like WHO. My focus is to limit the study to the actions taken by the government and BAT and perceive how both are playing on similar ground – discourses on environmentalism, for instance. Certainly, I do not intend to undermine the necessity of environment-friendly policies, but in the course of examining the discourses, it is merely inevitable to understand how these overt vocabularies help conceal some other power networks, no matter if they are preplanned or not. In this line, recent developments only helped the scope of this research.

A Concern Becoming Popular

Until very recently, neither the government nor any business agency in Bangladesh bothered about addressing environmental issues. It had never been a serious concern, in its modern connotation, from the 'public' desire either[3]. Roughly, the shift could be marked in the newly attained vocabularies, global in nature, since the early 90s (Steinberg 2003). One of the concerns is

---

[3] By 'public' I do mean the engaging agents in diverse issues. In a typical Southern nation like Bangladesh, they are a group of people surely from the urban educated middle class as it was discussed before. The concept appeared as a contested one during the past decades in social sciences and thus, needs to receive precision in each case. Also I meant to refer to the modern, because of the fact that more and more research in present days are showing the merits of the pre-modern ecology-equilibrium and people's knowledge on environment (for example, Shiva 1992). However, engaging to this kind of arguments would not be relevant in this endeavor.

surely manifested in the observation of the International Environment Day both by the government and the non-government agencies [NGOs], but it is the nominal one. Major concerns were revealed in the campaigning programs that took place occasionally and around the year. Mostly, the print documents, naming communication materials, and a number of NGOs – local and transnational – kept themselves occupied with campaigning for what they found as environmental consciousness and/or protection. As a matter of fact, a fairly good number of NGOs – for example, BELA, BAPA – only emerged within this defined new duty. Boosted by the proceedings, the national dailies also went for some issues. It was a time when the post of the cabinet minister of 'forest and environment' could be visible since he was the person who made the statements on the environmental issues, which were a major supply for the dailies' broadcast – a tendency since the early 90s.

Without a little exception, mostly this campaigning conveyed vague messages of 'keeping the environment alive' or 'protecting the environment.' Two of the major campaigners must be noted as the government of Bangladesh and BAT [then BTC]. The only concrete suggestion that was made was about plantation – 'plant trees' – though the urge meant to be a falsification of any assumed good intention or so. Both from the government and the BAT, the assertion of plantation was an irony. For the former, it is an irony because never was there a testimony of any intention to protect the forest reserves, namely the biggest ones in Sundarbans and in CHT, which has long been believed to be the subject of huge robbery[4]. For the latter, it is so because of their massive involution of the plain-land trees started back in the 80s to meet the burning and drying up the tobacco leaves – an act that had been unmarked till now.[5] However, whatever

---

[4] Sundarbans and Chittagong Hill Tracts [CHT] are the two most prominent forest areas in Bangladesh. Sundarban is located at the down south of the country, by the Bay of Bengal, whereas CHT at the south-eastern hilly part. It has long been discussed in the media that the forest woods are being stolen. The state officials, for the years, acknowledge the fact stating it as an act by the 'unidentified assemblage of the smugglers.'

[5] Right from the beginning of tobacco cultivation at large scale, the question of fuel never was considered a serious issue by the government. Due to the immediate profit, the local farmers and buyers used every possible wood in the north Bengal area (Chowdhury and Tauhid 2004). It caused a serious eradication of the local trees, vital both to the environmental safety and to the everyday needs of firewood for cooking. To mention the crucial fact, mango is one of the favorite and costly fruits in Bangladesh. Among others, mango and lichi trees were worn out in a large area of greater Rangpur, Dinajpur, Rajshahi, Pabna and Kustia. Hardly any suggestive literature is available that has taken the matter into serious account. One personal experience could also be an interesting supplement on this matter. Last year, asked by a local prominent development agency, I was researching on the social history of tobacco in Bangladesh. Though the research had very limited scope in terms of financial assistance, but we did come up with some

merits these communications immersed, it continued. Other agencies who were propagating similar kinds of messages were the emerging NGOs. With a closer look into the communication strategies by the hype of the developmental processes during the 90s, it is more likely to point out a distinct set of vocabularies related to the environment – both by the state authority and their counterpart for development mission, the NGOs. In a later phase, some other concepts like 'water pollution', 'air pollution' or 'lead poison' would accompany the concept of the plantation.

To my understanding, the recent move is the third major loud environmental step in a row taken by the central government. The first two were: a) 'banning' polythene for what was explained as polluting the environment by blocking the sewerage system and for the fact that it was not decomposed in nature; and b) 'banning' three-wheeler stroke engines, much used as public transport in the metropolitan areas, for what was explained as polluting the air by its hazardous exhaust. It is not incidental that all these are by the same regime of BNP, and all in a period of just three years (2001-2004). This action means to accrete my points to a firm position. That is to say, as I indicated already: first, responding towards what is supposedly conceived as environmental consciousness was never an urge earlier either from the state authority or from the public in general; second, speaking in a defined ecology-friendly way would, as I like to argue here, lead an authority to secure credibility in the present global context; and third, it could provide a political space beyond the credibility itself suppressing some significant issues.

However, compared to the previous ones, the recent step must be considered as a serious one. The immediate threat and danger that could take place as a consequence of the previous attempts is a nominal one. Besides the consumers' point of view, the respective stakeholders were not the giant ones in the Bangladeshi context. In both cases, some huge consumers were at stake without having the product. Being unable to provide a good alternative, the government had to take a serious risk with the possibility of public rage, especially in the case of polythene. To mention, it has been used as the sole packaging matter in everyday usage in shopping and wrapping for the last ten years or more. In the case of the three-wheelers, replacement with the gas-engine three-wheelers was made promptly, and actually, there was very little

---

fascinating results. But at the end, an international counterpart of the agency, a stakeholder of this research result, asked for reference on our note on tobacco burning. It was a ridiculous requisition since the mere fact was that no prior research could be found. The question appears to be a simple one. If tobacco production needed burning process around the cultivation field, and if there was no provision, facility or urgency made from the state authority, what else could be used for fueling the burning houses?

chance of public anger. But in both cases, nothing really happened as a result of public inconvenience. We need to be clear about how the discursive practices made up the public mind to the necessity of the change. Also we need to be spot on the role of the press. Far from the merits of such an environment-friendly stride, I am to pinpoint the obvious homework done long before the step was taken. This is to say the power of discourses on environmentalism, on a certain point, and not to undermine other discourses that combinedly enhance the governing model.

On the other hand, there were the manufacturers of polythene and importers of three-wheelers. The former was much more vulnerable than the latter. It was difficult for the small polythene bag manufacturers to switch to other professions, whereas the importers could switch to any other product to promote in the local market. But for an owner of a stroke-engine three-wheeler, having faced the ban, it was all of a sudden, a loss of almost 2 lac Taka (approximately $3500 back then) without being able to resell it. The only few examples show that a resale of some vehicles was possible outside Dhaka, which repaid only around one-eighth of what would be necessary to buy a new one. These insignificant facts have their influence in a larger scenario, as we will attempt to illustrate in the coming sections. To be sure of the significance of recent measures of tobacco control, it must be understood that BAT was one of the major taxpayers to the Bangladeshi government, let alone its supremacy of being a multinational agency with huge annual profits around the world. Apparently, the risk associated with this step is enormous. Then what made it feasible?

The Polythene and Three-wheeler Mockery

During the first half of 2002, just after the election, the newly elected government took charge, and a massive campaign began against polythene, or to be particular against the polythene bags. Almost in every governmental and state program, the necessity of the probable actions was explained thoroughly. Pamphlets were published; posters were glued on the wall; the public was preoccupied with speeches and their justification. National dailies reported asserting the importance of 'banning' the use of polythene bags, regardless if it was a self-renovated duty or a relaying as per guidance from the authority. The environment-related NGOs – from Oxfam to the local ones working in rural Bangladesh – seemed to be happy and found a considerate state apparatus behind this move. Senior academics and researchers were found to be seriously enthused, if not motivated, certainly most of who were the chemists. Understandably, a sense of comfort as well as dismay was generated in the course of the campaign. There was comfort, especially among the middle-class people, because already the message had been transmitted to a definite and defined audience. There was dismay, especially among the small traders and everyday buyers like the daily laborers, because the cheaper and easily available polythene bags meant useful accessories to them. Then, the products were banned, and the government was congratulated in every visible mode of communicative media for this gutsy role and their 'pro-environmental' stance.[6] The event was, interestingly, followed by the policemen's sudden intrusion into small grocery markets and harassment of the shoppers and buyers. It is hard to find any other consistent aftermath except for some new products of polythene bags in newer outlooks and presumably by some new manufacturers.

It is relevant to note, specifically in the current inquiry, that the entire polythene venture was maneuvered just on the backdrop of the huge turmoil of 'attacks on the minority people'[7]. Indeed, the redundancy of the mentioned venture, by and large, depreciated the obvious pressure of the continuous allegations against the government for not being able to control the hatred and anger against the 'minority', or, in some cases, for backing up the actions. Although these events are different, it is interesting to find, in the course of the field investigation, that the environment-related steps were taken by the ruling BNP at a time when they were under local and international criticism for failing any convincing explanation of those attacks.

Banning the polythene bags had some historical aspects too, which are to be taken seriously in regards to possible environmentalist hardware. The action was taken at such a time when the probable alternatives for packaging in Bangladesh had severely been damaged. There were two certain alternatives Bangladesh had earlier that could well meet the level of consumption. One was jute, and the other was paper. But both of them had already lost prosperity and were not in a situation to take over and supply the huge demand that appeared in the absence of cheaper and convenient polythene bags. It was no wonder that, except for the hype that furthered the credibility and image of the state authority, the banning was only a garrulous move that ended up with new, and

---

[6] I do mean here that, in the Bangladeshi context, any move seemingly 'popular', in terms of media responses and/or implementation, shocks the other major political party immediately. This has a particular meaning since the electoral outcomes are always swinging

[7] During the pre-election phase of 2001, started in October, there took place a series of violent attacks on the Hindu community in many places of Bangladesh. Investigations were done in different levels both within and beyond Bangladesh, except any convincing step by the following government of BNP. A strong hypothesis is there that the attack was pre-planned and executed expecting definite electoral responses out of fear towards some political force (source: reports in the dailies during the period).

relatively costly, polythene bags[8]. But there are the elegant manufacturing houses that produce mainly for upper-middle-class consumers, who continued with paper packaging – the outcome of this short-lasted propaganda. Some press coverage lighted on the matter as an 'eye-wash' and a 'failure', but that was not an effective move either.

Almost simultaneously, another campaign was launched against the stroke-engine three-wheelers. These kinds of vehicles had long been used as one of the popular forms of transport among the metropolitan middle-class people who did not have a private car. During the campaign these three-wheelers were mentioned to be polluting the environment for their dark black smoke. That is, smoke emissions from these automobile engines had the presence of dangerous levels of pollutants such as nitrogen oxides, hydrocarbons, and carbon monoxide. Unlike the previous one, this move entailed a serious re-organizing in terms of economic transactions. The lack of research, database or investigative journalistic pieces prevents any concrete figure of how many automobile three-wheelers were alive and used before the ban came to declare a sudden pull-out. Most of these vehicles were imported from the neighboring nation India with a few from the European nations. Without any state subsidy, it was commonsensical that the ban caused a serious economic disaster for the stakeholders, namely the owners of these vehicles. Yet again, no serious investigative reports were available that took a sensible account of the consequences. But there were some other stories, fragmented in nature, which came out and could give a better framework to comprehend the governmental action on what was propagated on an environmental ground.

As replacements for the banned items, new three-wheelers were strongly recommended both from the state-backed scientific research institutes, and precisely supported by some ecology-oriented NGOs. The main feature of these new vehicles is their gas-motivated engine. Since Bangladesh had a huge source of natural gas[9], the justification of introducing this kind of transporting medium gained common support. It is not unlikely that it took only a few weeks for the commercial fueling stations to be modified with the necessary equipment for delivering the gas. The state authority confirmed gas production and supply – refinement of natural gas for particular vehicle usage – through national corporations and private companies. Till the present day, the distribution of this

---

[8] Political economy of the abolishment of jute exclusively, and of paper partially could be a serious point of investigation in the research arena. Global power relations and the process of pre-defining regional markets seem to be significant components of the process.

[9] Bangladeshi gas resource has its own story to explore, mainly of gross manipulation in biding and distributing the sole authority to the multinational corporations. At the same time multinationals are also reported for causing a series of malpractices and violating human rights.

gas has proved to be chaotic and harassing for the recipients, the contract-based lower-class drivers who, in the near past, changed their skill and profession from stroke-engines to gas-engines vehicle drivers.

Yet the most exciting part of the whole venture was a separate one. Although very little investigation was done by the press and hardly anything appeared in the research literature, it is evident[10] now that the newly imported vehicles, again from India, resulted in huge profits for the importers. The ratio of profit exceeded any comprehensive framework and transgressed any business ethics, whatever that means. No official was charged for this serious manipulation and no step was taken even to conduct a state investigation. Instead, the circumstantial events suggested that the entire process remained officially unmarked. Banning the previous engines could only help a group of business agents to execute an unmarked profit-venture placing the consumer in a mandatory situation.

As I have mentioned before, I intend to explore the pro-environmental steps, both from the government and the business agencies, and to unpack the broader political significance of these actions. That the contemporary environment-consciousness amplifies the credibility, many of the undercurrent motions remain unmarked.

The Mighty Shrimp-Ghost

It has not always been the case with the mass people that they are not responding to a certain environmental situation, but rather the opposite. The above cases were the events, including the recent move of tobacco control, where the actions took place from the state authority as a bottom-down approach. But there were some significant events in contemporary Bangladesh, when the mass people urged for some governmental action to protect the ecological balance or responded sensibly to a possible attack on public health. These public calls were usually, without any exception, literally turned down with arrogant, brutal, in some cases, state intrusions in favor of the projects that were challenged by the masses. More often than not, the state interest was shown against the public interest, especially against the marginal people involved in manual jobs. Accordingly, it appears to be a mere fact that the masses and the state authority play antagonistically in regard to environmental and ecological issues.

The shrimp case could very well be the testimony of this claim. During the 80s, Bangladesh was discovered as one of the potential exporters of shrimp to

---

[10] Some estimated figures were available during the only discussions that took place. An engine costs 50,000 to 70,000 Indian rupee for retail sale in the Indian market and should be sold at approximately 1,00,000 Bangladeshi taka. On the contrary, as informed by the respondents, an engine costs up to 2,50,000 taka with some fare meter and so.

the world market. It was followed by the years of frog supply in a similar fashion. It should be mentioned that in the very climate and cultivation pattern of Bangladesh, frogs were believed to be ecology-friendly creatures of their insect-killing nature. The elimination of frogs caused some serious imbalance in the cultivating lands. However, the shrimp chapter has some serious implications and is comparatively an addressed phenomenon in the research literature (for example, Halim 2004). It needed the coastal area lowlands. The main idea of cultivating shrimps is to preserve salty water in the paddy-lands and then allow the shrimps to grow there. A systematic calendar is maintained, and strong supervision is continued during the process. Seizing of the lands used for shrimp cultivation has been a discussed issue in Bangladesh – mainly in public discussions and mainly in the small towns and respective localities – since, most of the time, it caused serious battles and bloodshed. The clashes are supposed to be among the local elites who fight for a single piece of land. Since shrimp cultivation is considered one of the most profitable ventures, the Southern part of Bangladesh witnessed numerous violent clashes among the traders. But this is not the sole conflict around the shrimp field. With a more sociological insight, one can be sure of the inevitable conflicting situation between the workers and the owners, their everyday resistance towards the hardship of life and uncertainty of the future.[11]

The growers' resistance has two distinct aspects considering the agricultural situation in Bangladesh. They are among the most marginal people, mainly the landless farmers, as it is defined both by the government and the development agencies. According to the legislature, Land Reform Ordinance of 1984 by the government of Bangladesh, an act that has its legacy from the land reforms that took place in the Pakistani period, of course with a series of disputes and as a result of proletarian movements, the abandoned lands must be redistributed to the landless farmers. Since most of the shrimp farms (*gher*, in local terms) occupied the abandoned lands (*khas jomi*, in the local term, refers to the land that was acquired by the government for redistribution), it meant clear denial of their claim. This way, the owners or the traders always managed either to produce the lease documents issued by the government or to demonstrate exclusive muscle power to drive their interest. In any case, there was no such evidence that the state authority challenged any shrimp trader. This has been an overt example of state manipulation and exploitation and has been the foremost cause for the growers to demonstrate. These facts were revealed in the field as the evicted people tried to file police cases and were rejected on the

---

[11] While there is a discontinued nature of information in the press, the subaltern forms of literature placed these incidents as one of the key dynamics of their expression such as verses or ballad kind of folk songs. For example, see Mridha (2000).

grounds of what the police defined as 'government paper' in favor of the traders. Ironically, a number of incidents were recorded, even by the lazy news-covering of the press, when police took brutal actions against these landless people. Besides the immediate response of losing their right, the farmers continuously are pinpointing to a separate issue. A land being used for shrimp-cultivation could seriously affect the productivity of other crops since the land immersed in salt water cannot produce the regular crops of Bangladesh. These coastal areas of Southern Bangladesh are especially famous for rice cultivation and cultivating rice is an utmost necessity for the poorest sect of the people. The government never took any measures to protect the paddy fields from the profit-making ventures. On the contrary, the state authority responded brutally to silence the uprisings. One of many of these uprisings drew a larger attention as the press covered the event. It was in Satkhira, in the southern part of Bangladesh, where an outrageous protest took place in 1997, and one woman, Zaheda, was killed by the police (Mridha 2000). Not surprisingly, even this protest could not resist the deal – a contract between the government officials and the shrimp-farm owner, an influential rich person from the locality. Daily newspapers, though partially, kept on reporting these happenings on a routine basis during the mid and late 90s. Still, this kind of information is available mainly through the small and alternative dailies about how the lower-strata growers would demonstrate and get tortured and then, without any alternative, would join the same farm as a daily laborer.

While we are considering the state actions on environmental grounds or the policies that are supposedly claimed as ecology-friendly, we must critically look into events like the one mentioned above. The shrimp laborers are reported to protest here and there against the occupation of their rights, against the abuse of the paddy fields. There have also been numerous reports of suffering from severe infection in workers' skin due to direct contact with the salty water. None of their protests or health concerns, though poorly investigated and lacked proper references, could make the state authority rethink, or respond to, the urgency of the matter. However, shrimp case is being cited here as an event of the recent past to juxtapose the contradictory attitudes by the government and, truly, by the NGOs too. But the jeopardy of governmental actions is not limited to it only.

It would be interesting to list and look further at some more acts that can be comparable in regards to how the state policies respond to a certain situation and how most responses are not 'ecology-friendly', or with a sensible public health concern. I would like to mention here three different acts from the state government. First, the establishment of an Eco-Park project initially in the

Khasi[12] area, and then with renewed enthusiasm, in the *Mandi*[13] area. Eco-park is a development project mainly to attract tourists. The idea is to acquire a huge land primarily from the *Khasi* area and transform it into a park which would be what the officials refer to as an ecology-friendly place. Ironically, the *Khasi* or the *Mandi* people were already living in a 'natural' atmosphere, and the project could only evict them from the land. In both cases, local people protested in every format. Unlike some regular events, this was not overlooked either by the press or by the NGOs. Major dailies, including *Prothom Alo* covered the situation along with the NGOs' participation in the protests. The civil society activists and the left organizations also demonstrated their criticism and anger. Their main point was that the government was becoming greedy and looked only for their financial profits. Scientific essayists, in support of the protests, illustrated the aftermath damages to the natural equilibrium, let alone the invasion of an indigenous habitat. In brief, everything possible was done to sensitize the government; further attempts to pressure the government legally and beyond also ended up with the same result. Second, the unprecedented blast that occurred in 1997[14]. The foreign company that was supposed to bear the responsibility, Unocal (then Occidental), was never under any serious pressure by the government. Further, they were just gifted with allocations of more gas blocks for commercial production. Third, the abuse of natural forests in the Chittagong Hill Tracts [CHT] in the Southeast part of Bangladesh, and the initiation of rubber plantations. This is also an event that lacks proper attention from the press. It should be mentioned that the CHT has been under state surveillance for years as the ethnic minority population is always struggling for their rights, and it is said that the landscape is also a subject of manipulation. While the habitat had its natural forest, a twofold business venture is being inspired – relentless consumption of the woods, mostly by the state-backed settlers from the dominant Bengali ethnic group and military, that leaves the hills a graveyard, and rubber plantation that is likely to make soil disintegration.

---

[12] Khasi is an ethnic population living in greater Sylhet district. Some modest reporting could be found at - http://www.sdnbd.org/sdi/news/pages/eco-park/eco-park.htm

[13] Academically known as Garo since the British colonial administrators, *Mandi* is the local name of an ethnic group living in greater districts of Mymensing and Sylhet. The ongoing project of Eco-park in this region appears to be with modest concern, but mostly remained a 'regional' issue even to the international bodies supposedly concerned of such matters. An appeal against the project could be seen at – http://www.omiusa.org/JPIC2003/BangladeshPark.htm

[14] In Magur Chara, north-eastern part of Bangladesh, a huge blast took place in 1997 in the area where Unocol, a transnational corporate company was exploring gas and oil. Again it is a pathetic example of under-actions taken by the government and civil agencies, and under-coverage too by the media. For some details, see – http://www.gasandoil.com/ogel/samples/freearticles/roundup_04.htm

This discussion does not refer to any conspiracy theory in particular, nor do I ever suggest that any particular government has an explicit approach against the environment. Instead, what I really mean is that the policies of different governments hardly differ. One can notice that in most of the cases, a new government is just carrying out, if not fostering, the legacy of the former. In this line of discussion, I intend to seek attention to the critical and complex nature, often contradictory, of the state authority. It is necessary, I argue, to comprehend the multifaceted relationship between the state and the business agencies and the engagement or disengagement of the international social organizations. I think it is just amateurish to engage with the apparent meaning of the pro-environment activities. Bangladeshi governments were never in a position to respond to the shrimp factor on a public ground. Never were they willing to address the ecological damages or, for instance, the danger of public health issues. It is, then, necessary to analyze how the environmental discourses, the rhetoric of certain surface global knowledge, help to take shelter behind it and conceal some deeper political ties. The final two sections in this chapter, in brief, would be engaged in an attempt to consolidate my reading in this regard. It is a difficult process on the backdrop of a lack in the research literature and in the research interest too, and only with the field experience of a single research project. How the profit-making types of machinery are day by day forming an oligarchic entity is one of my basic searches these days. I urge you to consider my attempt to bridge between the potential research on undercurrent political processes and the research on environmental and ecology matters in Bangladesh.

Public Health Revisited

Understandably, the emphasis that is being asked for from the diverse recipients while reading the recent call is the obvious concern about public health. The effectiveness of the call overrides any possible political turmoil or process – to put it modestly – whatsoever since the seeming opposition is BAT, a giant multinational corporation. Necessarily, the call is a provocative one. It provokes, on the one hand, the jubilation from the civil camps acknowledging a valiant move, while on the other hand, the accreditations from the transnational agencies like WHO, of course with prior guidance from other guru agents, for being on the 'right track'. Further, it provokes, significant, at least locally, responses from the opposition local party while they are likely to be at a loss. We should be careful of the enormous capacity of these activities around the globe. It happened to be a discursive formation of what environment-friendly steps should mean. Last but not least, the ban provokes a reaction from BAT, notably the principal tax-payer in the economy. The final one surely had been measured thoroughly before the announcement took place, no matter what it really might cost to the annual transaction of BAT, or how the announcement would be put into action, except for some public harassment in dispersed events as it had happened in the recent past.

From the state's point of view, the last visible public health concern revealed was regarding the AIDS and HIV threats in Bangladesh. The possible threat had never been understood properly due to the contested facts and figures placed by the government and the non-government agencies (Chowdhury and Gulrukh 2000). Manifestations from the government, though, were loud. It had a twofold scheme. Firstly, defying any serious threat to the Bangladeshi population and justifying the position with the moral and religious values of the masses. Secondly, allowing campaigners as many as possible to launch their 'AIDS-related' programs.[15] Finally, it turned out to be the promotional activities for the production and selling of condoms[16].

Against the backdrop of the immense threat of arsenicosis, a disease caused by the elevated amount of arsenic in drinking water, while more than 80 million of the population is under serious threat[17], any serious resolution is still unfound. It is merely unconvincing that the research findings that suggested what are believed to be 'safe water options' have not been implemented yet. Yet, the most significant aspect is its political implications on a global scale. The Bangladeshi government never once thought of challenging the transnational agents who were supposed to be responsible for the disaster. It is being said, though loosely, around some marginal research circles that the disaster is an outcome of the extra consumption of soil water; hence, the promotion of deep tube wells and irrigation needs to be under scrutiny. It was agents like UNICEF who aggressively promoted tube wells as the sole option for drinking water all over the nation during the last three decades. The transformation was established at the cost of the abolishment of all kinds of traditional sources of drinking water that are, in present days, ironically, mentioned as presently. It must also be noticed that the business ventures for bottled water appeared at

---

[15] Mostly they were communication programs, hence printing and broadcasting campaigning materials that enhances 'awareness', according their terms, regarding AIDS and HIV infection (Chowdhury and Gulrukh 2000).

[16] At least one cabinet minister can be quoted in this regard. While inaugurating the first ever condom factory in Bangladesh by the Bangla-German Latex Company, the then health and family welfare minister hoped that foreign companies would follow this example and start more condom companies. News in *The Daily Star*, Dhaka, 12 September, 1999.

[17] Though without a hope yet, the crisis is being acknowledged from different corners within and beyond Bangladesh. But we must be careful that there is only a very few, if any, attempts made to historically, and critically, analyze the role of the transnational development agencies in demoting the traditional ways of drinking water which is now proved to be as safe options. Here is a site for some basic information: http://www.sos-arsenic.net/index.html

once and the process is being nurtured by the state authority. It appears that the government barely found a way of promoting privatized water, surely for the well-off people.

I argue to pursue here regarding public health. That is, there has been a subtle shift in governmental concerns over public health issues in recent years. Far from securing public health needs on an individual scale, the current tendency is to address it environmentally. More often, the connotation of asserting an environmental cause even transgresses tangibility and involves a vague meaning.[18] In brief, my point is that the discourses on environmentalism are occupying the space of what was conceived as public health. This proposition insists on a serious political explanation. In a democratic framework, public health had been considered as a subsidized area from the state, regardless of the actual situation over the years. While exclusive privatization is taking place in the health sector, and only a little space is left for the mass people, it is the concept of 'environment' that is replacing the probable 'charitable' areas. Further, I would like to contend that the government responds environmentally only when this seems to be profitable for some business groups, and the ways it responds utterly outlines, or validates, a route of profit-making for some groups.

Invading Farming Lands in the North-Bengal

The major land resource for BAT (and former BTC) has long been the North-Bengal part of Bangladesh, including the greater districts of Rangpur, Rajshahi, Dinajpur, Pabna and Bogra. During the late 70s and early 80s, the then BTC launched serious campaigns to make the farmers interested in tobacco cultivation. The methods employed in this venture – from selecting lands to collecting quality leaves, from establishing purchasing centers to presenting awards to successful agents – could best be defined as the contemporary idiom of 'aggressive business strategy.' The specific features of the lands in the northern part of Bangladesh endorsed their business. To mention the fact, within years, BTC almost monopolized the entire tobacco production. It is hard, though, to legally define the lands as occupied by the company since a distinct form of contract farming was set, and BTC could only be identified as the buyer. The whole process was maintained under strict supervision by the officials of BTC and the local purchasing agents. Agricultural inputs for the tobacco industry have been a confined area until very recently.

---

[18] For example, in the early years of AIDS-campaigning in Bangladesh, the government officials frequently referred to the concept of "social environment". Understandably, it was associated with morality and values.

In very recent years, the dry soil of the northern part attracted at least two different cash crops other than tobacco – tea and corn[19]. It is not possible, due to the lack of research or journalistic reports till now, to take a sensible account of how it is affecting the overall tobacco production, or for instance, the interest of BAT. However, taking a clear account needs precise agro-economic baseline surveys and it is too early to assess an economic account since the shift is at its early phase. But the ignorance about the new ventures, academically, I consider, is annoying.

The striking feature of the recent ventures is that some business groups succeeded in 'buying' thousands of acres of land. On a personal tour, I managed to identify three different companies trying to build tea-estates, two of which started production while one started marketing, and one company got a lease of hundreds of acres of land for cultivating corn. This is something found in just two districts – Panchagar and Lalmonirhat – and quite in a touristic fashion without any prior intention of researching the issue[20].

Corporate Production of Political Vocabularies

This is where the current search could be posited. I am insisting on the fact that research on covert power pools in Bangladesh is painfully insufficient. Further, research or even journalistic reports on the new business ties and ventures are not available either. The only accessibility in regards to the present inquiry can be made on research on environmental issues – about the damages and probable ways out. While I am aware of the usefulness of this kind of research, I am much doubtful about the technicalities that are deployed in producing this set of knowledge. Typically, these attempts conceal, at the first stage, any possibility of broadening up the scope of conceptualizing the issues in a socio-political framework. On the background of such an atmosphere, it is hard to proceed with a research agenda I am trying to uphold. It is the rigorous anthropological research method and deductive analysis that helped assimilate the observations in this chapter.

---

[19] There is a growing industry of chips and flakes in Bangladesh. Among the metropolitan consumers, these are exclusively favorites. Also there are some imported brands. It is more likely, as I sense, that some multinational brands would be locally produced in a few years.

[20] I traveled for two short trips during April and June of 2004. The initial idea was to look around and search inspiration for my 'literary' pieces. Somehow the findings were shocking for me since I had no prior knowledge of this huge transformation. I cannot remember any visible news reporting on this and checked it with others. Yet the most shocking thing is the 'agreement' that must have been done between the government and the respective companies. I mean to say that these pieces of land were categorically government-owned – hence the *khas* land – and should have been redistributed amongst the landless people according to the existing law (Land Reform Ordinance 1984).

I renounce to accept the environmentalist blabbers from the business groups as they are uttered. The chapter could have been anticipated, in regard to their overt activities regarding environmentalism, as to be an assessment of the discourses propagated by a single multinational company on the issue. The recent situation just urged on some different points to look at. But this is merely a commencement of the necessary research tradition to be made in the future to unpack the complex business ties, intersecting interest groups within and across the national border, and, more importantly, the effective usage of environment-related vocabularies in championing their interest. This is of utmost necessity, I believe, for a better understanding of the contemporary political processes. I am not in the position to see the recent banning as an action that is executed on environmental causes. Rather, my position is to view it as a validation of some other acts not yet marked properly.

Chapter 7

The Power of Translation

Although influential donor agencies like the World Bank had always been keen to compel the Bangladeshi government to remodel the educational system, the government of Bangladesh had been hesitantly responsive toward the policy suggestions until the early 90s. The hesitance can be observed by examining the historical interaction between the government and the World Bank during the previous period. The shift is understandably related to the neoliberal ideologues around the globe. Initially, the policies primarily focused on primary education and later expanded to include other levels. From the policy agents' point of view, the urge had its assertion compatible with what they had long been propagating around the world, especially on the onset of apparently populist policies in some of the developing nations. On the other hand, the government's denial had much to do with the general attitudes towards privatization and, accordingly, the basic principles that the Bangladeshi state had upheld right from the beginning. However, the implications of the state's denial of the external recommendations need to be read critically rather than its apparent meaning whatsoever. Even the general attitude towards privatization, as it is believed to be an antagonistic one, should not be taken for granted. Within less than a decade, the emergence of private universities as a space for materializing undergraduate and graduate education marked the success of the ventures. Apart from its credibility as a viable business venture, these institutions are relishing the shift in the discussion level – from a mere alternative for the disqualified candidates at the public universities' admission exam to a vivid avenue of a competitive and modern educational package. The utmost characteristics of the private universities' education are being said to be of international standards, an undefined perception of arguably a lifestyle statement around the world. It appears to be a conformist appreciation of the categories and concepts of contemporary modernization. This chapter seeks to examine the discursive formation of 'private' in regard to the higher education scenario in contemporary Bangladesh.

In Search of a Background

It is of utmost importance to note that the Private University Act[1], which accredited private universities as a useful and desired venture, took place at a time when Bangladesh was arguably going through a transition towards democracy. The military dictatorship of Lt. Gen. H. M. Ershad (1981-1990) was over through a popular urbanite uprising just nearly two years before. The elected government in 1991 took over the responsibility to maintain Bangladesh in what the Western and local press defined as the democratic process. Whatever merits or demerits this move entailed should be treated in a deeper understanding of the educational policies and objectives of a typically southern nation like Bangladesh and in accordance with the external influences along with its local agents. In the later phase of this discussion, I hope to explore the concept of translation, as it was illustrated by Talal Asad[2], which would provide a comprehensive understanding of the relationship between the policy agents and their recipients. This is not to say, however, that the changes in attitudes of the state organs toward the privatization of higher education were a sudden event and manifested without any prior groundwork. Instead, what I would like to say is that the groundwork had long been done. Further, I would like to maintain that compared to its predecessor, the government, supposedly entitled as a democratic one, had an extensive space to execute it.

Given the fact that the admission-seekers have been huge in numbers, the state-financed universities, what I would call public universities from now on, were a place of extensive competition. Although there were some visible attempts to increase the number of public universities and affiliated colleges with similar provisions to offer distinct undergraduate and graduate programs[3], they were far behind the actual need. While I am arguing this, it must be clear that the question of need also demands to be explored further. Here, some factual points could be useful. The higher education system in Bangladesh typically,

---

[1] 'Private University Act', Act No.34 of 1992, Published in Bangladesh Gazette Extraordinary, Dated 9th August, 1992. Could be seen at: http://www.sai.uni-heidelberg.de/workgroups/bdlaw/1992-a34.htm
[2] Talal Asad and John Dixon provided a different conceptualization of translation that went beyond the conventional literary meaning of it (Asad and Dixon 1985). Another document by Asad is equally, if not more, relevant. See Asad 1995.
[3] In the Bangladeshi context, on the onset of British colonial education policies, it meant until very recently Bachelor Honors course for three years and Master for one year. The recent readjustment is to add one more year in the Bachelor Honors program. This is an ongoing process. Eventually, the Master program appeared to be a subject of much confusion. Hypothetically, public institutions are still running one-year Master program and they are having the potentials of heading toward nowhere at the end. The level of confusion and lack of guideline is just too high in the current phase.

includes the universities along with the university-affiliated colleges that provide education after higher-secondary (up to grade XII) education. As already mentioned, the universities used to be public, i.e., government-owned and monitored, until 1992. Facts and figures often are misleading to assess an approximate account of the education system in Bangladesh. It starts with the defending tendency of the literacy rate. For example, the 2001 census shows that the rate is now about 48%. But this type of representation is from the actual scenario and provides only very little for comprehending it. Instead, this is a kind of action that responds to the policies of big agencies like the World Bank. According to recent data (2003) of BANBEIS [Bangladesh Bureau of Educational Information and Statistics], there are only 22 public universities in Bangladesh in comparison to the 52 private universities. In both cases, these are the official figures, and can hardly be measured on real ground. Out of the 22 public universities at least 12 were declared within the last three years and still are defined in the papers.

On the other hand, some initiators just filed applications and managed to receive approvals for their private universities. Further, there appeared to be little criticism about the failure of the government to monitor the quality and essential facilities of a university. So, the government has been trying to discard some of the private universities that have already appeared, at least on the papers. Yet again, the UGC [University Grants Commission] record is yet to show any sign of discarding. In recent years, almost 1,50,000 students have mentioned getting enrolled in higher education. The number is increasing every year. Still, public universities (along with the affiliated colleges) are covering more than two-thirds of the total students, a fact that demands to get noticed in the hype of private universities. So, one can look back into the question of the 'need' and rethink. The actuality of the 'need' should be seen as grounded on the fact that the state has been believed, in the popular mindset, as solely responsible for the expenditure of education.[4] This very approach, from the people's point of view, has to do a lot with the onset of the emergence of Bangladesh through a kind of populist uprising and in turn its adoption, as a state, of socialism as one of the columns in the first constitution after independence. The government of Bangladesh, regardless of its inclination,

---

[4] By and large, the expectation of the mass has been largely ignored in the conventional research projects, mainly conducted by the donor agencies and within their project framework when they had to deal with the Bangladeshi educational policies. But that is altogether a different issue.

needed an overt attempt[5] to maintain the demand. Despite the differences among the political parties and the turmoil that emerged right after the independence, the state authority has been officially inclined to manifest education as a people's right, hence a subject of government subsidy.

Contrary to the situation, it should also be clear that the upper-middle class people in the city area long back started advocating the idea of purchasing higher educational facilities. The fact is revealed, subtly and indirectly, in their continuous venture of sending their offspring to the Northern universities. Apart from the little financial aid and support, this drift meant to cause a crucial level of investment from the respective families. How this specific kind of investment in their children's education is structurally a part of the domestic budget and reflection of the aspiration is a crucial issue embedded into the history of class formation and nuclearization of family. With an overriding influence of *Bilati*[5] education since the colonial period, the desire for foreign education is an inevitable feature of the upper-middleclass people. Surely, this should be seen only as a part of many manifestations of their mobility. The self-motivated expenditure for higher education by an influential sect of society only gives us a sense of justification for the later official move. More often than not, before private universities were established in Bangladesh, a common excuse became evident among the well-off people's daily discussion about the pointlessness of paying overseas universities the money they had been spending on their children. One must notice the obvious provocation of this assertion in the domain of what tentatively could be defined as patriotism in the era of investment and economic growth. I intend to perceive this discursive field as a strong lead toward privatization in the later years. It is, however, interesting to note that there is no such evidence available that the growth of private universities caused any decrease in the number of overseas students from Bangladesh. This is mainly because the target groups for private universities vary in their objectives. A portion of the students are enrolling in the undergraduate programs of private universities to make an avenue for the universities abroad at the graduate level. On the other hand, other students are into it just because

---

[5] Comparable to 'foreign', as discussed in chapter 3, *Bilati* is an adjective of the word *Bilat* referred mainly for the then Great Britain, the colonizer of Indian subcontinent. Having been awarded a degree from Britain, especially in law, literature and natural science, was regarded as a fundamental trait both to assure the elitist life style and to secure the *avant-guard* progressivist position. Emerged in the colonial era, the term later referred not only to Britain but as a generic one to anything related to the West. But the linguistic shift is an interesting fact to notice. That is, the affluent people hardly use this term these days, rather prefer an English word for this.

they were not able to secure any place in the public universities. In the end, well-off families have more options to switch between top-rated private universities and universities abroad. It can also be noted here that some of the capable private universities maintain administrative and business links with a handful of Western universities – i.e., Victoria University in Melbourne or London Metropolitan University, etc.

Crises and Scopes for Approaching Education as an Area

Among others, the major methodological crisis for education research is its discontinuous nature, especially in Bangladesh. The kind of work considered as the genre of research belongs to the high-profile donor agencies who schematically conduct either what they define as the baseline studies, or the evaluations. Hardly do these staff deal with the social consequences or engage with the historical processes. In other words, these research projects are grounded on the macro frameworks of development and continue, pathologically, to meet the prior figures set long before by some transnational development agent. Further, it is almost impossible to locate any such research that supposedly is trying to unpack the critical nature of the classed society with a remarkable effect on the educational policy in a given time and site. Also, it is a crisis that research based on discourse analysis is very limited in number. Research that roughly could deal with public discussions ends up as a pathetic example of a 'perception study.' This is not something exclusive to research on education, but it is a generic tendency in development research of contemporary Bangladesh. So, it is an utmost hard attempt to anticipate critical research on higher education in Bangladesh.

Another problem, I anticipate, lies in the fact that the privatization drive has long been associated with educational ventures other than categorical higher education, which cannot be taken within the scope of the current exploration. First of all, primary (from grade I to V), secondary (from grade VI to X), and higher secondary (grade XI and XII) education had been a subject of privatization long before the private universities began to flourish – a fact that claims to have relevance in the current search. Besides, numerous posh elementary schools of different kinds – namely kindergarten, nursery, pre-cadet, preparatory, and so on – have firmly been established for at least the last two decades. These are targeting, nonetheless, the middle and upper-middle class people in the city areas. For secondary and higher secondary schooling, the initiatives were mostly from the private sector. Yet, sector should not be the right word to use here. Against the backdrop of the British colonial administration in the Indian subcontinent, the urge for modern education became apparent. People in the countryside with well-off peasant backgrounds and willing to do charity activities were the first ones who established the schools. While this had been a general trend in the rural areas of colonial Bengal, the urban space was covered by the migrated-*jamindars* and emerging traders – both in Kolkata (then Calcutta) and in Dhaka. Long before a formal state-controlled system was set, historically, these have been the ways to substantiate a modern desire. But the university-education was always a different issue. What for years had been providing a foundation to claim the merits of privatization in higher education is necessarily of significance in the current investigation.

To be precise about the aim of this chapter, once again, I would like to underline that this chapter is a modest attempt to analyze the huge shift in the perception of private universities, as well as in their representations, over roughly a decade. Eventually, the work is to unpack the public discussions, hence to realize the discourses in a certain context. Instead of what a dominant educational system is providing to its recipients, the main concern is to problematize how it is being portrayed, manifested and constructed in the public mind; how its features are being asserted as the norm; and how the construction of private universities in its process is discarding the credibility of public universities, eventually, diminishing its potentials as a source of knowledge, whatever that means. This is of utmost importance since it is the space where the concrete authority of this business venture lies.

Translation as a Conceptual Tool

To proceed with my argument, the concept of translation is very important. Unlike the conventional meaning of the concept in the genre of literature and linguistics, Talal Asad illustrated it in an entirely different way. Engaged with some of the early anthropological works, Asad and Dixon (1985) went beyond its apparent meaning. Asad argued that the process of translation, when it takes place in the colonized people, went far beyond the simple act of translating words or concepts, specifically when the source of translation is the colonizer itself.[6] Instead, he furthered, it had been a process of translating the historical structures, a concept he explored for investigating translation as a social process. In other words, it is a series of systems – like parliaments, families, police, bank, insurance even values and norms – along with the concepts and categories that are being translated towards the recipients' location. Even when a typically linguistic translation is concerned, it is not the colonizer's language that needs to make the adjustments and to accommodate at the end, but the colonized people's language, as Asad contends, that has to accommodate the necessary changes within it to meet the requirements of the translation process.

---

[6] Asad (1995) op.cit.

In this chapter, Asad's concept of translation is relevant to the extent that the establishment of private universities has been embedded into the meaning of desired international education within the categories and concepts that are overriding in a local situation.

The concept of 'ideological state apparatus', introduced and illustrated by the renowned French Marxist scholar Althusser is another relevant insight to explore in the current issue. According to Althusser[7], the modern state is not only on the RSA [repressive state apparatus] like police, criminal justice, and prison that force the people physically, but also on the ISA [ideological state apparatus] like educational institutions, legal systems, religions, politics, arts, sports etc. These are the institutions, as he argues, that generate ideologies that the individuals internalize and act according to. Grounded on Gramsci's concept of civil society[8], Althusser's work underlined, unlike the dogmatic Marxist, the importance of ideology as a structure that would discipline the individuals.

The Early Formation: Discourse of 'Scarcity'

The establishment of private universities in Bangladesh was founded on the logic of the lack of sufficient educational institutions. This particular stance marked the impression of private universities in the early years of the emergence of private universities in the early 90s. The sudden rise in the number of private universities in very recent years was not even seen as a possibility at that point. To be precise, there are more than 50 private universities currently registered under the UGC [University Grants Commission, a governmental establishment to administer the universities], most of which came out in the last 4/5 years. In reverse to that, it took almost five years to increase the number to five after the first-ever private university in Bangladesh started in 1992. Initiated with the North South University, arguably the most influential among all, there were Independent University and *Gono Vishyabidyalaya* in the first three years. It seems that the Private University Act came out as a hurried adjustment to the necessity of issuing a release for the North-South University authority to launch as a venture. The governmental document is also a testimony of how they felt inclined to react to the initiative as an act to 'meet the increasing demand'. As it states in the clause:

> Whereas it is necessary to establish private universities in order to meet the *increasing demand* of, and to extend *pervasively*, higher education in the country, to facilitate the access of the *general public* to higher education and to create in this way a class of skilled persons; and whereas

---

[7] See Althusser 1978.
[8] See Gramsci 1973.

several *well-wishing* persons, associations, charitable funds and institutions of the country are eager to establish and manage private universities; and whereas it is expedient to provide for the establishment of private universities (Private University Act, 1992, italics added).

The above passage is self-evident of how the state repulsed the question of privatization, on the economic or business ground, when it comes to education. 'Increasing demand' is a phrase here to refer to the inadequacy of higher educational institutions, though in a vague manner. The urgency that is manifested here never reveals the cost of education in private universities, no matter if there are a number of people who can afford it. Generally, only the tuition fee in any of the prominent private universities is around 1 lac taka (roughly 1500 USD) per year, which surpasses the total amount of a class-one government official's annual income. On the other hand, public universities charge a token amount of money as tuition fees and charge some extra fees for examinations etc. Nonetheless, the most striking phrase in the document is 'general public'. On the one hand, the phrase juxtaposes the capability of the marginal middle-class people with the affluent upper-middle-class ones which inevitably seems to be absurd. On the other hand, a close examination of the situation could reveal that it was founded on the fact that the private universities were still to achieve any academic credentials by their name. It is meant to be the secondary choice for the probable consumers of private universities with the prime choice of any of the public universities, including the technical ones (medical or engineering). In other words, off-springs of the well-off background who failed to secure a place in the public universities might have decided to go to the private universities, as a viable alternative to the overseas universities.

More often than not, the failure to secure a place in a state-financed university, even after being backed up by a place in any of the private universities with a huge tuition fee[9], was considered a disappointment. It was expressed in such a manner. Though it needed a critical examination of the public discussion to notice, the sense of insecurity was very much there. Getting admitted into a private university necessarily meant a clear deprivation – of not being able to have the 'best' educational institutions, hence the public universities. The only possible compensation could be in the form of majoring in a suitable discipline. Interestingly enough, there was hardly any variety in the disciplines, and the list would entail – business studies, economics,

---

[9] No meaningful comparison is possible. Whereas a public university charges a token amount of tuition and examination fees, a private university charges from 50000 to 200000 BDT per annum for covering tuition and materials.

communication, environmental studies and, very soon, medical studies. Limited available subjects only indicate the inner mechanism of the big agencies about how they had foreseen the changes in professionalism. Except for environmental studies, all of these subjects were already believed to be professionally lucrative including those of business studies or administration, economics, engineering and technology, and medicine.[10]

Despite the early struggling phase, the private universities – both as an administrative system and as a knowledge production house – gained enormous authority in the coming years. Indeed, within a very short period, the idea of private universities set the standard of higher education in the public imagination. The transformation necessarily had an intermediate phase engaged with its public counterparts. Within a sharply constructed dichotomy, the public university got pathetically driven away.

The Take-over Phase: Undermining the Public University System

As I discussed in the methodological section, the discontinuity in the research literature causes serious problems in comprehending the situation. The phase that I like to name as the 'take-over phase' is largely characterized by its deliberate series of activities to undermine the public university as a system of education-provider. While it is a critical task to explore the responsible events in an absorbed fashion, it is really hard to distinguish the actors of this undermining process. They are subtle and incidental. Actualities in the public university campuses were surely of concern. But at the same time, media activities severely affected the public perception of the public universities, obviously in a negative manner. Roughly, the period of this phase could be determined from the mid-90s to the end of the decade. I would like to identify and propose three features that came into the gross middle-class mindset as evil about the public universities during the period. Those are: a) student politics, b) medium of instruction, and c) inefficiency. Even though public universities are still the major places for seeking higher education for the broader middle-class people, I would like to argue they as the decisive ones for demolishing the image of it. These are the crucial threads, I maintain, for

---

[10] This is an area which needs separate attention to unveil the interconnectivity of the different actors. A tentative list could entail transnational donor agencies, local policy makers, international consultants and their local counterparts, financiers and industrialists and other masterminds of a particular time. Interesting enough, the transnational NGOs have started looking for the environmental experts these days. It cannot be seen as an increasing consciousness about environment, rather an insistence from the donors to incorporate these experts for what they define as 'proper' research. In this line, the private universities were able to foresee the consequences in the development field.

generating and perceiving an indefinite idea of the international standard of higher education, eventually the international education, which appeared to be an advertising strategy for the private university initiatives in the later years.

a) Student politics got to be portrayed as anonymous to the concept of terrorism and destruction. It is very interesting to notice that its credibility marked score even until the recent past when it was considered one of the major forces to combat the military regime. All of a sudden, just after the democratic electoral process was initiated in Bangladesh, it was pointed out as the evilest part of public university campuses. With a few exceptions, the press media became the most vocal advocate of such ideas. A party-neutral president[11], along with his civil society masterminds, played a crucial role in this issue of the campaign against student politics. Very typical of the subcontinental situation, the student organizations have long been subjects of state manipulation and sabotage. During the 50s, the then-Pakistani ruler formed NSF to destroy the democratic and anti-government students' movement in the universities. The trend, by and large, is still on. Regarding the manipulative power game the state nurtures, the simplistic charge against anything named student politics seems uncritical and helps to demoralize the spirit of public universities.

b) Medium of instruction, contrary to the previous one, never was a point of criticism in the press overtly. Rather, it was initiated within the desire of the affluent middle-class people to get into the global arena. Along with the previous one, it generated serious dissatisfaction among the guardians. Right from the beginning, the independent Bangladesh urged for the importance of the Bengali language as a medium of instruction in the universities. The 1973 University Act underlined its priority clearly, where public universities were believed to be the nurturing place for the Bengali language as the medium of instruction. Keeping in mind the linguistic basis of the Bengali nationalist movement, this article meant a lot to the sentiment of the vanguard people of that time. Accordingly, the dissatisfaction that I am talking about seems to be obscure and undefined. Further, a number of disciplines, including business studies, computer sciences,

---

[11] During the Awami League rule from 1996 to 2001, ex-chief justice Shahabuddin Ahmed was elected as the president. He was considered as a non-bias person to the political parties and was one of the major architects of civil society – a forum of vanguard middle class intellectuals and professionals propagated for what they perceived as human rights and democracy.

economics and so on already started a kind of English instruction in different universities. This can be clearly defined as the transgression of the act. But in reality, this course of action is praised and is a point of the initiator's pride.

c) Inefficiency is another point of accusation against public universities. It seems to entail both administrative and academic capabilities. With a close investigation, first as a public university teacher for more than ten years, and then purposively engaging with the teachers and students of private universities, and again being in specific field investigation from February to August in 2004, I could find the complex nature of the claim. On the one hand, it indicates the systematic lethargy that the public university administrations gained due to a number of reasons – the lack of monitoring, the manipulative employment and direct influence by the governmental agencies. While at the other hand, it points out the overt nature of the state intervening in teachers' grouping that affects the process of teachers' employment and the selection of vice-chancellors. Last but not least, the claim puts a finger on the incapability of checking students' violence on campus.

This is not to say that any of the claims are unjust, given the contemporary public university situation. These claims could gather a series of evidence from the recent past of the universities. My intention, by any means, is not to defend the public universities as they are at present. Instead, what I like to insist is the very nature of the representation of the public universities is necessarily conditional to the representation of the private universities. While the portrayals of the state-financed institutions entail all the negative connotations, it certainly leaves space for the private ones to get authorized with the positive connotations. Further, the process of representation is not an unconscious act, nor is it an incidental one. Accordingly, this is a dichotomy neatly executed, no matter if it had been a prior conspiracy. In this line, my arguments do not intend to defend an imaginary ideal of public universities or to defy the allegedly set accusations against them. I, at best, am trying to unpack the styles of representation of the public universities, and the aftermath of this formulaic representation as a justification of, and a subscription to, the private universities.

Ironically, till the present day, a major portion of the teaching staff is being recruited from public universities – mainly on a part-time basis. Further to this fact, it is also interesting to notice that the administrators are also coming from the same origin – mainly the retired teachers and/or administrators along with the retired civil and military bureaucrats. While the major daily newspapers are full of contributions and commentaries from the same kind of academics, paradoxically, they tend to show little confidence in the public universities as a system. Earlier, I mentioned that the media played a crucial role in the negative portrayals of public universities. I think the audio-visual media, namely TV, should be considered as crucial in this line. Given the huge popularity of this media and a hyped urge to exhibit campus life in the popular genres of TV productions, it appeared to be merely an influential process to undermine public universities. Understandably, not all the projects were deliberately meant to be instruments against the public university images. At the same time, the shallow emotionality and intellectuality embedded into the construction of the campuses failed to regenerate any serious implications for the universities, especially in the era of the privatization ideology.

A Case to Assert My Identity as a Teacher

A discrete one, this event could be an interesting lead toward an understanding of the mass media's crude role in depicting public universities. The funny part of the story made me think over it again while I was engaging the issue here. It was sometime in 1997. I was working at my university office at dusk. My colleagues were gone. Two old familiar faces appeared at my door. They were senior to me while I was a student at the university. Both of them made dramas for the TV. They came to shoot a play that demanded some classroom scenes and were looking for a place for the cast to change costumes. Soon, I found two TV stars and a team of crews behind them. I decided to avail them my room as a green room. After a few minutes, while I was reading a book sitting in the corridor, the producers came to me asking if I was ready for an on-spot shooting in the classroom since they were short of a cast in the team. Well, I was ready to the extent that I loved acting for years. But I asked about the role. The role was that of a university teacher lecturing his students, including the 'hero' and 'heroine'. They were supposed to communicate some pranks, believed to be gestures of their affection and romance behind the teacher's eye – a scene not very uncommon. The teacher was expected to be tight-lipped, and with a kind of dumb personality. I refused to take the shoot. "What's wrong? You're already a teacher," the producers asked. My position was clear: "That's the main reason. First, I have never been a tight-lipped teacher. Well, I can portray it only if the story has enough reasons to promote it, which is not the case. And although I have no serious problem with my students doing romance, it is hardly possible in my class to communicate among themselves in this way. Again, I have no problem characterizing a teacher this way if I find the story strong. And finally, since I believe that there are plenty of dull-headed teachers in the universities, I find no reason to portray one of them." My senior university-mates found me arrogant. Actually, we had a bitter argument about the last point. They tried hard but could not see why I found the teacher unimpressive since he was delivering the proper lecture, and they were not trying to make fun of him. I offered them to be in my class, of course, arrogantly. Finally, the resolution came from a theatre-loving boy who was around. He happily played the role, according to the director. Before leaving the campus, the director-producer pair suggested that I be more practical.

I do not mean to assert too much in this case. This case refers to the series of casual representations of university campuses and agents in the more popular forms of cultural products, which, I argue, not only weakened their credibility but helped the private universities to secure authority at the common level.

Discourses of 'International Education' and 'Competence'

With a huge number of private universities in recent times, it is now evident that they are doing good business. The level of financial investment is high. How they manage to make it a profitable venture is now far beyond any general observation. A critical investigation could reveal that the accounts of a private university are not as straightforward as they seem to be. There are diverse partnership and exchange programs that secure the income of apparently a risky establishment like this. Also, a major shift took place in terms of the specialization they are offering. A range of courses from liberal arts and social sciences are being offered. However, though these developments are of significance, the scope of this study conceals furthering on these issues. My main concern here is the vast shift in the credibility of these institutions. Unlike previous years, no one has to feel the pressure of not being able to find a place in a public university. Instead, the situation is just the opposite. Getting admitted to a private university is grossly referred to as one's status, and well-off families quite often deliberately allocate such budgets for their children.

How an undefined and ambiguous conceptualization of the 'international education' took place is an interesting query to explore. It is not a simple process of qualifying a specific educational package only, but a process of dismissing the state-backed educational institutions at the end. At the same time, it is not a fight between two distinct pedagogical schools. Instead, one must be aware of the fact that contemporary public universities could hardly be defined as a sad mimicry of bunches of ideas. And they are not being able to manifest the objective of education on a populist level. However, it seems most unlikely that an active challenge might come shortly.

The agents portraying private universities as a system are complex and exclusively intermingled. In the previous section, I attempted to briefly sketch the style of representations of public universities, which, I contend, played a crucial role in idealizing the 'quality' of private universities. Discourses of 'international education' and 'competence' could be identified as crucial to this huge shift. Grounded on the same discursive formation, these discourses largely overlap each other. Roughly illustrating, the common sense is that the main aim of education is to make the students 'competent', and that is what an 'international education' means. Concepts like 'skill', and 'quality' could best be seen as codes of a specific lifestyle far away from that of the public university campuses and are deployed to substantiate the main thesis of 'competence.' Competence is crudely perceived through the jobs and financial returns.

While the private universities, transnational development agents, and business groups across the national border have a close tie – officially and beyond – the myth of competence through international education must be challenged. What I would like to propose, briefly, is to see the question as a translation of the global system in the Bangladeshi locale. And the mighty system is named development. Private universities are ideological apparatuses not as such of the state, as Althusser (1971) argued, but for the global system of development and trade, and most probably for the trade of development.

Chapter 8

Conclusion: Will Popular Be 'Popular' Again?

The title put here appears to be entirely an isolated one to what all other previous chapters tried to point out. The actual purpose of this proposition, however, is just the opposite. Rotating around the central arguments, this thesis attempted to trace different kinds of popularizing projects – all within a range of similar motives – in various areas. These motives, with sheer focus, carry out the mission of making the 'popular'. It is of utmost importance to identify this mission as a cultural as well as a political one. While it is cultural in the way the projects are launched and manifested and seek to amplify certain meanings, political in terms of implanting certain domination over its subjects. In many ways, as the arguments and observations proceeded on in the chapters, the state agencies are apparent in their role to realize the popularizing projects. On the other hand, corporate groups are simultaneously identified as the authors of these projects. The relationship between the state agencies and the corporate groups should be seen as oligarchic. In the concluding chapter, it is, thus, my intention to propose that discovering the 'popular' is becoming more important for corporate groups nowadays, and it does not necessarily cancel out the role of the state but rather takes it as a *de facto* ally.

This book, initially an outcome of a designated research, has proposed three central arguments – both at the conceptual and experiential levels. Those are: 1. Being popular in Bangladesh is neither an arbitrary process in the end, nor can it be understood with the classical model of popular vs. elite culture. Instead, making it popular is one of the central projects of the contemporary power network. 2. It seems to be necessary, from the rulers' point of view, to bridge between the imaginary locales of the people with the ruling machine. By a generic term like 'rulers', I mean the nexus of several agents and organizations – governmental and state organs, the finance and business groups, the media network, which is collaborative with the former ones, and the underworld associates. 3. Popularizing projects can be seen as active and conscious attempts to generate and/or regenerate discourses that are believed to entail potential, yet inadequately measured, space. Accordingly, the 'popular' is a set of forms and ideas that are the outcome of these production systems.

Still, some areas should seriously be considered when I am preparing my 'research' as a book, or booklet in the precise term, whatever the distinction means. The first concern is the relevance of this manuscript in contemporary Bangladesh, or the contemporary world, assuming a broader readership once it is published for a global audience. My second concern is about my ever-growing apathy toward what is being defined as 'research', precisely because of their patrons and purposes in a given juncture to set terms for 'scholarly' practices for becoming hegemonic. My third concern is about the legacy of the concept of 'popular' in academia and how we would deal with the orthodox political implications this concept has been entailing for decades. Fourth, and perhaps the most troubling concern is about the positionality of the military as a social-political agent in Bangladesh.

Starting with the last one, I seriously opine that military force has had a serious impact on Bangladeshi political space, specifically since the assassination of Sheikh Mujibur Rahman in 1975, followed by a number of military coups. Saying so, the military has not always been an overt actor, nor is it a serious point of reference in academics or polemics. I tried to recall the reasons for keeping this factor much subdued in the body of this book. The primary reason is obvious and involves the security concerns of any author. But given my legacy as a polemicist in Bangladesh, even in the local language, it should not be a convincing reason in the end. The fact that journalists and academic practitioners maintain a huge silence about this defining force leaves us with little to no choice of engaging this tendency as a 'dataset'. One could wonder about this silenced nature of academia and journalism, but that is exactly how the Bangladeshi intellectual space is made up. At the same time, this is a characteristic I would love to explore further in my future endeavors, and is not entirely a Bangladeshi phenomenon, not anymore in the neoliberal world where 'security' as a hyped discourse provides an extended space for the military force in many nation-states, and is very 'popular'. More and more, it is becoming the foundational particle of the nexus I referred to here.

With an elaborate understanding of my fourth concern, other concerns fall into the right places and need very little explanation. This work remains relevant, though it could have received an engaging readership had it been published years back. Similarly, my third concern also reasserts the importance of studying 'popular' in specific cultural-political locations. Perhaps I would like to clarify a little more about my apathy toward 'research', the second concern mentioned above, before recapping the chapters in this book. My apathy toward 'research' has been a political understanding of the relationship between assigning/governing bodies, both local ones and international ones, and academics in a given (research) project. While I am not referring to something out of the blue, and there are the voices across the globe, specifically from the Global South, more evidently from the practitioners of disciplines typically defined as liberal and social studies, but an overt assessment of the prejudices and disparities of the 'research industry' is not what is a common practice. I think that the 'publishing industry' has been dictating terms of research and academia and often presupposes what it defines 'research' as the determining factor of academia. I am aware of the fact that my understanding cannot be substantiated with a minimal paragraph or two, and needs serious references for putting forward. But my intention is not to persuade my readers in line with my understanding but to explain why and how my journey, as an academic and/or 'researcher', has been troubled as I had to continuously deal with the established parameters and perceptions of 'research' and I could not find much in those. I took my time, I had to, and then decided that it was never about being defined as a 'researcher'. For me, it has always been to make sense, to attain clarity. This is how I could reopen the question of the significance of 'popular' in a reconfigured cultural-political space, understandably with a deflected meaning from its orthodox resonances.

Recapping

The introductory chapter brought a brief historical background, my understanding of the concepts and issues, and a fragment of the initial research design. One major objective of this chapter was to underpin the central debate about 'popular' and 'people' in social scientific knowledge. Chapter two provided some analyses of the instrumental strategies that were in use in Bangladesh during and after the regime ruled by the military dictator Major General Ziaur Rahman. The military-dictator-turned-into-public-leader Zia, can be seen as a crucial icon in the cultural processes of Bangladesh, something that would be shared by different political corners, regardless of their inclinations, but apparently with different projected consequences. Instead of being engaged with the strictly defined political processes, I attempted to understand the iconizing process. Inspired by what Stuart Hall (1988) had illustrated thoroughly in regard to the British society in Thatcher's regime, the observations put in this chapter served as a thread towards the importance of propagating ideas and broadcasting images. Zia – both as an icon and a set of ruling strategies – is seen here as the instigator of the process, a crucial one for modern nation-states. As an icon, I consider that he was, and has been, a crucial combination of 'youth' and 'American', that transcended the temporality and political groups and projected in MacGyverish fantasy.

The third chapter examined how consumerism and commodities are central to identity formation. Launched to target middle-class consumers, the project should be seen beyond its obvious meaning of business. In this line, as the main line of argument has come out in this chapter, the assertion of new goods, forms and ideas leads towards a certain lifestyle. Consumerist culture is a generic term to grasp the processes, as it were. Besides the advertising language and images, the process of popularizing consumerism and goods is a complex project from different actors, and in different phases. While certain features should exclusively be understood in the contemporary arena, there are certain historical threads too that tend to signify a set of meanings, albeit regenerated and modern. One binary that appears to be central in this meaning-construction process is that of 'local and foreign'. Considering the structural meaning of these two, they both serve as specific kinds of referents to the mentioned lifestyle. This chapter underlined identity formation as a major area of the making of popular, hence a consumer identity. The next chapter, the fourth, attempted to analyze and explore a crucial aspect of the political process in recent Bangladesh. With special reference to the political discourses and probing into a single case, it unmasked the secular prejudices. It was a major case. The astonishing removal of the then-president of Bangladesh, Mr. Badruddoza Chowdhury, did not invite any sensible discussion in the public. The public here necessarily should be perceived as the educated middle class who, without much exception, are the main readers and play a crucial part in organizing the opinion and thus, formulating consent. Given a parliamentary democratic structure, the president is always hypothetically a subject of intervention. Still there had not been many examples like this where the parent political party decided to remove such a major official whom they had earlier selected themselves. The apparent absurdity of this move had to be legitimized, at least for generating the consent of the fellow people loyal to the party. So, stories were made up about how he transgressed the defined honor of Zia, the already-mentioned founder of the ruling BNP. This is where the main argument of this chapter was rotating: the undercurrent political processes are systematically ignored in the media and thus in the middle-class psyche, and the overt analyses revolve around the flat and simple dichotomy of fundamentalism and secularism. The systematic distortion of, or reluctance to, the undercurrent events reduces the possibilities of conceiving or designing political actions that could entail the interests of the majority.

The next chapter, about cinema production and its creation of meanings related to the 'nation', dealt with a singular case yet again, like the previous chapter. This time, the case is taken from what is repeatedly referred to as mainstream films. It is important to note that the general middle-class reaction towards mainstream films, in Bangladesh, has long been very negative. In general, they find 'distaste' and 'vulgar' in these loud and melodramatic audio-visual products. The scenario is very different from the attitudes generated by similar products in the neighboring country, India. Accordingly, the films in Bangladesh are largely produced for the urban working-class people and the marginal income group of people in the small towns. In this sense, this has something specific to do with the generic concept of mass. The chapter illustrates how the recent film production tends to restructure images of the 'hero' and fascinatingly blends the prejudices of the modern nation-state. This is a tendency that cancels out the previous principles of depicting the heroes, of course, within a similar masculinist ground, which was likely to attain more kind of Robinhood-like activities. Films must not be seen as a general referent to a range of productions in the cultural industries, especially at a time when cinema in Bangladesh has been experiencing a serious downfall. My main proposition here is that the film productions, or visual production in broader terms, seem to be a testimony of how the concept of nation has been asserted both in subtle and obvious manners. This chapter, conceptually, can be seen closely tied with the chapter on consumerism, though exemplified in a different context.

Chapter six is again an endeavor to explore the political vocabularies. This is about the hype of environmental consciousness shown in the actions of the government and some social organizations. The purpose of this chapter is to look beyond the apparent meaning of these actions, claiming much popularity among a particular class and propagating the popularity to go beyond the class boundary. The entire scenario is much more complex than it appears to be and needs to be penetrated to reveal its connection with the global course of action and ideas. Concerning some actions necessarily against what is said as environmental consciousness, this chapter attempts to reinterpret those actions. It also sheds light on the intricate nature of adjustments from the business agencies to remain with a popular public presence in a changing situation. The main argument that I tried to pose here is that the systematic publicity of some ideas that already have some global connotations is an effective measure to construct and claim popularity. It has nothing to do with the actual doings, nor does it even remain at risk of being challenged. Rather this kind of publicity seems to be schematic and provides a defined space to bring in collaboration between the state agencies and the corporate groups, secured with the already-materialized popular support. The next and second chapters have dealt with the tendency of privatizing education, evident during the mid-90s. Although a significant portion of primary and secondary educational institutions have been private for years in Bangladesh, the recent trend is to incorporate the higher education sector. There are further significant differences. In Bangladesh, private institutions have been playing a crucial role in fostering formal education in marginal and peripheral areas. But the mentioned recent trend is about planting higher education as a market service and making a profit out of it. That is, however, not the main concern of this chapter. With a more careful reading of the situation, it could be revealed that the privatization of education is not merely a process of tangible establishments, but rather a pointed mission of undermining the public educational establishments and popularizing the private ones. Consequently, it is structurally related to one another – promoting images of private higher educational institutes and demoting the public ones.

The process entails a set of vocabularies, hence discourses, like international standards or educational qualities, which are propagated in the media and take place as consent.

Popuganda?

In a nutshell, this book has aimed to illustrate how the popular is not an arbitrary outcome as it is claimed to e, and how the project of constructing the popular is functioning with subscriptions from different agents. With the popularizing process in various forms, there can also be seen a subtle tendency of making a national-popular, in its more orthodox fashion. By agencies, I intended to include simultaneously the governmental and state agencies, the media and the corporate groups, while state agencies are a complex mixture of civil and military bureaucracy, something hardly seen by other analysts of our time. Different agencies should not be perceived as discrete categories but as overlapping in many aspects. Further, what I am trying to pursue is these agencies share similar missions, create space to collaborate and, regardless of some disputes among them, maintain an oligarchic relationship. This is the flexible yet definitive location of the popularizing project – a cultural mission of the ruling systems.

Engaging in different areas of cultural production and discourses, I tried to trace a line of manufacturing the popular. It is expected that the importance of exploring the popular would be perceived in the social scientific exercises. Concerned with a particular location, this body of work denies the flat and essential understanding of popular culture and, in turn, posits the question of 'the popular' within a complex web of social agencies. At the end of this journey, the most important question could be why it is so necessary to construct some meanings that tend towards the association with, or reflection of, the people. This question might have been encountered with a rigorous set of conceptual and methodological tools that include the multilayered issues of nationalism. However, this particular book did not cover this area extensively, and I am not happy about that. I paid serious attention, while preparing this manuscript, to the possibilities of analyzing nationalism with a deeper understanding. That felt like a different project altogether.

Also, this study could not succeed in exploring the process of making a national-popular to its optimum possibilities. Related to the previous section, the aim had to do with the examination of particular cultural forms that claim authentic national culture. The study, however, started with the promise of approaching this. However, the immensity of the queries was a serious concern for keeping that in a single study. Yet again, the more I was into my study, I had to voyage through many cultural sites in different social spaces to make sense of what I was looking for. The production of cultural forms and codes taking place in different sociocultural spaces has almost a singular pattern of popularizing process. As a 'researcher', my inability to access first-hand data of some agents' activities is something that needs to be mentioned – especially the activities of the military headquarters in a given Southern nation named Bangladesh. This inability may read crucial, especially in the era of overwhelming empiricism, although I preferred to rely on deductive methods throughout, a rigorous method that is being squeezed in the advent of the 'research industry', especially in the fields of liberal studies. For me, there is no better way to go beyond the apparent meanings and perceive the nuances of any social situation except the "implementation of the principle of *reflexivity*" (Bourdieu 1993, 264).

It is an interesting question to exercise and finish this book: why is this that some very potent agencies, who can do whatever they like, and they do them too, maneuvering plenty of ways, need to sanitize them with a tag of 'popular'? Why is it the case that they relentlessly propagate ideas that otherwise do not even wait for approval from the public, especially in a Southern nation location like Bangladesh? I know the answer, perhaps, again with a rigorous deductive way of knowledge (or maybe wisdom). It is about the perception of people in a given governing structure, the remaining ruin of the conventional political thoughts that have no functioning implications but weigh the pale relic status of the yesteryears. My answer should be augmented in yet another piece of work, I understand. 'Popuganda' may read light in context, but could well be the title of that imagined work, with a fitting subtitle as 'Earning Compatibility with the Text-book Politics'.

References

Ahmed, Rahnuma. 1999. "Women's Awakening: The Construction of Modern Gender Difference in Bengali Muslim Society." In *Contemporary Anthropology*, edited by In S. M. Nurul Alam, Ainoon Nahar and Manosh Chowdhury, 109-132. Dhaka: Department of Anthropology, Jahangirnagar University.

Ahmed, Rahnuma and Chowdhury, Manosh. 1997. "Lingo, Sreni Abong Onubader Khomota: Bangali Musolman Modhdhobitto Poribar o Biye (Gender, Class and Power of Translation: Bengali Muslim Middle-Class Family and Marriage)." *Shomaj Nirikkhon*, 63: 1-33.

Ahmed, Rahnuma and Chowdhury, Manosh. 2003. *Nribigyaner Protham Path: Samaj o Sanskriti*. Dhaka: Ekushe Publications Ltd. [in Bengali].

Althusser, Louis. 1971. "Ideology and Ideological State Apparatuses: Notes Towards an Investigation." In *Lenin and Philosophy*, 127-186. London: New Left Books. [also New York: Monthly Review Press, 1978].

Anderson, Benedict. 1983. *Imagined Communities. Reflections on the Origin and Spread of Nationalism*. London: Verso.

Appadurai, Arjuna. 1986. *The Social Life of Things: Commodities in Cultural Perspective*. Cambridge: Cambridge University Press. https://doi.org/10.1017/CBO9780511819582

Appadurai, Arjuna. 1988. "Introduction: Place and Voice in Anthropological Theory." *Cultural Anthropology*, 3.1: 16-20. https://doi.org/10.1525/can.1988.3.1.02a00020

Appadurai, Arjuna and Breckenridge, Carol A. 1988. "Why Public Culture?." *Public Culture*, 1(1): 5-9. https://doi.org/10.1215/08992363-1-1-5

Appadurai, Arjuna. 1990. "Disjuncture and Difference in the Global Cultural Economy." In *Global Culture: Nationalism, Globalization and Modernity*, edited by Mike Featherstone, 295-310. London: Sage. https://doi.org/10.1177/026327690007002017

Appadurai, Arjuna. 1996. *Modernity at Large: Cultural Dimensions of Globalization*. Minneapolis and London: Minnesota University Press.

Asad, Talal. 1961. *Some Aspects of Change in the Structure of the Muslim Family in the Punjub Under British Rule*. Oxford: University of Oxford [unpublished B.Lit. thesis].

Asad, Talal and Dixon, John. 1985. "Translating Europe's Others." In *Europe and its Others*, edited by Francis Barker et al., Vol. 1, Colchester.

Asad, Talal. 1988. "A Comment on the Idea of Non-Western Anthropology." In *Indigenous Anthropology in Non-Western Countries*, edited by Fahim Hussein, 284-289. Durham: Carolina Academic Press.

Asad, Talal. 1992. "Conscripts of Civilization." In *Civilization in Crisis*, vol.1 of Dialectical Anthropology: Essays in Honour of Stanley Diamond, edited by Christine W. Gailey, 333-51. Gainesville: University of Florida Press.

Asad, Talal. 1993. *Genealogies of Religion: Discipline and Reasons of Power in Christianity and Islam.* Baltimore and London: The John Hopkins University Press.

Asad, Talal. 1995. "A Comment on Translation: Critique subversion." In *Between Languages & Cultures: Translation & Cross-Cultural Texts*, edited by Anuradha Dingwaney and Carol Maier, 325-332. Pittsburgh: University of Pittsburgh Press. https://doi.org/10.2307/jj.10677896.25

Barnard, Alan, and Jonathan Spencer, eds. 1996. *Encyclopedia of Social and Cultural Anthropology.* London and New York: Routledge.

Bourdieu, Pierre. 1993. "Concluding Remarks: For a Sociogenetic Understanding of Intellectual Works." In *Bourdieu. Critical Perspectives*, edited by Craig Calhoun *et al.*, 263-275. Chicago: The University of Chicago Press, 263-275.

Brosius, Cristiane. 1997. "Mapping the Nation." In *Mappings. Shared Histories. A Fragile Self*, edited by Pooja Sood. Delhi: Eicher Gallery.

Burling, Robbins. 1962. "Maximization Theories and the Study of Economic Anthropology." *American Anthropologist*, 64, 802-821. https://doi.org/10.1525/aa.1962.64.4.02a00090

Carrier, James G. 1996. Consumption. In *Encyclopedia of Social and Cultural Anthropology*, edited by Alan Barnard and Jonathan Spencer, 128-129. London and New York: Routledge.

Chomsky, Noam and Herman, Edward S. 2002. *Manufacturing Consent: The Political Economy of Mass Media.* London and New York: Verso.

Chowdhury, Manosh and Gulrukh, Saydia. 2000. *AIDS O Jounota Niye Discourse: Rogir Prantikota* (Discourses on AIDS and Sexuality: Marginality of the AIDS Patients). Dhaka: Rupantor Prokashona.

Chowdhury, Manosh. 2000. "Shonabondhur Piriti Ebong Bhalobashar Shushil Discourse (Subaltern and Liberal Discourses of Love)." In *Shamprotik Nribigyan (Contemporary Anthropology)*, edited by S. M. Nurul Alam, Ainoon Naher and Manosh Chowdhury, 97-108. Dhaka: Department of Anthropology, Jahangirnagar University. [in Bengali].

Chowdhury, Manosh. 2001a. "Shukkho Premer Ortho: Nimnoborgiyo Ganey Jounota o Narir Attoshotta (The Meanings of Love: Sexuality and the Female Subject in Subaltern Songs)." In *Chorcha: Nribigyaner Probondho Shongkolon (Practice: A Collection of Writings in Anthropology)*, edited by Zahir Ahmed and Manosh Chowdhury, 55-64. Dhaka: Department of Anthropology, Jahangirnagar University. [in Bengali].

Chowdhury, Manosh. 2001b. "Cholochchitre Osleelota Proshongo o Shyamlaler Golpo (The Issue of Vulgarism in Films and the Scapegoat)." In *Shahitya, The Daily Sangbad.* [in Bengali].

Chowdhury, Manosh. 2003. "Bangladeshe Civil Shomaj: Mohanogor-Modhdhobitter Goshthibodhdhotar Noya Probonota (Civil Society in Bangladesh: Oligarchy of Metropolitan Middleclass)." *Jogajog.* [in Bengali].

Chowdhury, Manosh and Tauhid, Hossain. 2004. "Social History of Tobacco [Ad]Venture." [Unpublished research report]. RED-BRAC and WHO.

Dagi, Ihsan D. 2002. "Islamic Political Identity in Turkey: Rethinking the West and Westernization." Research monograph, Budapest: Center for Policy Studies, Central European University.

Dwyer, Rachel and Pinney, Christopher. 2001. *Pleasure and the Nation: The History, Politics and Consumption of Public Culture in India.* Delhi: Oxford University Press.

Featherstone, Mike. (ed.) 1990. *Global Culture: Nationalism, Globalization and Modernity.* London: Sage.

Fiske, John. 1989a. *Understanding Popular Culture.* Boston, MA: Unwin Hyman.

Fiske, John. 1989b. *Reading the Popular.* Boston, MA: Unwin Hyman.

Fiske, John. 1992. "Popularity and the Politics of Information." In *Journalism and Popular Culture*, edited by Peter Dahlgren and Colin Sparks, 45-63. London, Newbury Park and New Delhi: Sage Publications.

Forgacs, David. (ed.) 1999. *Gramsci Reader: Selected Writings 1916–1935.* London: Lawrence and Wishart.

Fortes, Meyer and Evans-Pritchard, Edward E. (eds.). 1940. *African Political Systems.* Oxford: Oxford University Press.

Foucault, Michel. 1989 [1972]. *The Archaeology of Knowledge.* London and New York: Routledge.

Gramsci, Antonio. 1973. *Selections from Prison Notebooks.* Trans. and ed. by Q. Hoare and G. Nowell-Smith, London: Lawrence and Wishart.

Halim, Sadeka. 2004. "Marginalization or Empowerment?: Women's Involvement in Shrimp Cultivation and Shrimp Processing Plants in Bangladesh." In *Women, Gender and Discrimination*, edited by Kazi Tobarak Hossain, Muhammad Hassan Imam and Shah Ehsan Habib, 95-112. Rajshahi: University of Rajshahi.

Hall, Stuart. 1981. "Notes on deconstructing "the popular"." In *People's History and Socialist Theory*, edited by R. Samuel, 227-240. London: Routledge and Kegan Paul.

Hall, Stuart. 1988. *The Hard Road to Renewal: Thatcherism and the Crisis of the Left.* London: Verso.

Hall, Stuart. (ed.) 1991. *Representation: Cultural Representations and Signifying Practices.* London: Open University Press and Sage.

Hall, Stuart. *et al.* 1978. *Policing the Crisis: Mugging, the State and Law and Order.* London: Macmillan.

Hall, Stuart and Whannel, Paddy. 1965. *The Popular Arts.* New York: Pantheon.

Hayat, Abul. 1987. *Bangladesher Cholochchitrer Itihash [History of Films in Bangladesh].* Dhaka: Film Development Corporation.

Hesmondhalgh, David. 2002. *The Cultural Industries.* London: Sage Publications.

Hossain, Golam. 1988. *General Ziaur Rahman and The BNP: Political Transformation of a Military Regime.* Dhaka: University Press Limited.

Leclair, Edward E., Jr., and Harold K. Schneider, Harold K. (eds.) 1968. *Economic Anthropology: Readings in Theory and Analysis.* New York: Holt, Rinehart and Winston.

Marx, Karl. 1976 [1876]. *Capital.* Vol. 1. Translated by Ben Fowkers. London: Penguin Books.

Mridha, Kanal Lal. 2000. "Zaheda Hotyar Kobita [Poetry on the Murder of Zaheda]." In *Kortar Shongshar: Naribadi Rochona Shongkolon [Master's House:*

Anthology of Feminist Writings], Saydia Gulrukh and Manosh Chowdhury, 322-327. Dhaka: Rupantor Prokashona. [in Bengali].

Mukul, M. R. Akhtar. 1982. *Ami Bijoi Dekhechhi*. Dhaka: Jatiyo Shahitya Prokash. [in Bengali].

Nandy, Ashish. 1985. "An Anti-Secularist Manifesto." *Seminar* 314.

Pinney, Christopher. 2001. "Introduction: Public, Popular, and Other Cultures." In *Pleasure and the Nation: The History, Politics and Consumption of Public Culture in India*, edited by Rachel Dwyer and Christopher Pinney, 1-34. Delhi: Oxford University Press.

Polayni, Karl. et al. (eds.) 1958. *Trade and Markets in the Early Empires*, New York: Free Press.

Ritzer, George. 1996. *The McDonaldization of Society: An Investigation into the Changing Character of Contemporary Social Life*. Thousand Oaks, CA: Pine Forge Press.

Ritzer, George. 1999. *Enchanting a Disenchanted World: Revolutionizing the Means of Consumption*. Thousand Oaks, CA: Pine Forge Press.

Ritzer, George and Stillman, Todd. 2001. "The Modern Las Vegas Casino-Hotel: The Paradigmatic New Means of Consumption." *M@n@gement* [Special Issue: Deconstructing Las Vegas], Vol. 4, No. 3, Toronto, University of Toronto, 83-99. https://doi.org/10.3917/mana.043.0083

Sahlins, Marshal. 1972. *Stone Age Economics*. Chicago: University of Chicago Press.

Shiva, Vandana. 1992. *The Violence of Green Revolution: Third World Agriculture, Ecology and Politics*. London: Zed Books.

Sparks, Colin. 1992. "Popular Journalism: Theories and Practice." In *Journalism and Popular Culture*, edited by Peter Dahlgren and Colin Sparks, 24-44. London, Newbury Park and New Delhi: Sage Publications.

Spencer, James. 1996. "Formalism and Substantivism." In *Encyclopedia of Social and Cultural Anthropology*, edited by Alan Barnard and Jonathan Spencer, 242. London and New York: Routledge.

Standing, Hilary. 1991. *Dependence and Autonomy: Women's Employment and Family in Calcutta*. London and New York: Routledge.

Steinberg, Paul F. 2003. *Understanding Policy Change in Developing Countries: The Spheres of Influence Framework*. Global Environmental Politics, Vol. 3, No. 1, The MIT Press. https://doi.org/10.1162/152638003763336365

Talbot, Ian. 1998. *Pakistan, a Modern History*. New York: St. Martin's Press.

www.ingramcontent.com/pod-product-compliance
Lightning Source LLC
Chambersburg PA
CBHW070336230426
43663CB00011B/2341